# Quarterly Essay

Quarterly Essay is published four times a year by
Black Inc., an imprint of Schwartz Books Pty Ltd.
Publisher: Morry Schwartz.

ISBN 9781863954051 ISSN 1832-0953

Subscriptions – 1 year print & digital
(4 issues): $79.99 auto-renewing within Australia
incl. GST. Outside Australia $134.99. 2 years print
& digital (8 issues): $159.99 within Australia
incl. GST. 1 year digital only: $49.99.

Payment may be made by Mastercard or Visa,
or by cheque made out to Schwartz Books.
Payment includes postage and handling.

To subscribe, fill out and post the subscription
card or form inside this issue, or subscribe online:

**quarterlyessay.com**
subscribe@blackincbooks.com
Phone: 61 3 9486 0288

Correspondence should be addressed to:

The Editor, Quarterly Essay
22–24 Northumberland Street
Collingwood VIC 3066 Australia
Phone: 61 3 9486 0288 / Fax: 61 3 9011 6106
Email: quarterlyessay@blackincbooks.com

Editor: Chris Feik
Management: Sophy Williams
Production Co-ordinator: Caitlin Yates
Publicity: Anna Lensky
Design: Guy Mirabella

| HIS MASTER'S VOICE | The Corruption of Public Debate under Howard |
|---|---|

David Marr

> As the clever hopes expire
> Of a low dishonest decade …
> —W.H. Auden

## THE OLD VOLTAIREAN

The habits of luxury hotels are hard to break. Though Saigon is now the communist metropolis of Ho Chi Minh City, the best hotels cluster where they always have, around Lam Son Square. There in the Park Hyatt John Howard faced the Australian press in November last year. The event was low-key: no podium, no flags and little time. These were the last hours of the Prime Minister's first visit to Vietnam and his motorcade was about to leave for the airport. Howard had called the press together to plug nuclear power and farewell Ian Thorpe from the pool. He was relaxed. A week of hobnobbing with the leaders of APEC had climaxed late the night before in a restaurant where the Bushes and the Howards feasted alone on crabs and lotus-seed soup. The President paid.

David Speers from Sky News caught the Prime Minister's eye. "Just before you leave Vietnam, can I ask you, do you think the Vietnam War was a mistake?"

Someone had asked at last. From the moment Howard arrived in Vietnam, he had been lavishing praise on the communist regime. He spoke of the Vietnamese as people after his own heart with "entrepreneurial flair and spirit" committed to "the role of small and medium-sized enterprises." He imagined a future in which Australia and Vietnam were "forever linked in the fastest-growing area of the world economy." One night at an Asialink dinner, he made a vague allusion to the war: "Australia's relations with Vietnam have, of course, gone through a number of iterations." It's an awkward word for ten years of combat.

Once the Howards and their entourage travelled south from the APEC meetings in Hanoi, the war was everywhere. They lit incense at a cemetery for the war dead of Vietnam at Go Cat. They drove in convoy to the rubber plantation at Long Tan where eighteen Australians died in a single night of fighting forty years ago. John Howard laid a wreath and expressed a few regrets: not for the 500 Australians, the one and a half million Vietnamese military and the two million civilians who died in the war. To a handful of Australian veterans gathered at the white cross that marks the battlefield, Howard acknowledged the shabby treatment soldiers had back home when they returned from the fighting. "We won't make that mistake again."

Speers woke next morning thinking it odd that no one in the press pack had asked Howard – simply and directly – what he thought of the war. "He had been telling us a lot during the week about the success of Vietnam and the great opportunities it afforded for Australian business," he told me. "But the question of the war hadn't been raised." This seemed particularly odd because of the obvious parallels with Iraq. "I must confess it didn't strike me until the day we were leaving that, hang on a minute, does he still think that fighting the Vietnam War was the right thing to do when the rest of the world has moved on?"

Howard took his time answering Speers' question. He was thinking it out carefully as he spoke.

> I supported our involvement at the time and I don't intend to recant that. I believe that in public life you are accountable for the decisions that you take. I mean, I didn't hold any position of authority then, but I supported the reasons for Australia's involvement and nothing has altered my view that – at the time, on the assessments that were made then – I took that view properly. And I don't intend to indulge this preoccupation that many have in recanting everything that they supported when they were in positions of authority.

Journalists glanced at one another. Was he bagging Malcolm Fraser? Or perhaps Robert McNamara, the former US secretary of defence who now says the Vietnam War was "wrong, terribly wrong"? Howard wasn't naming names. His point was that conceding the truth isn't his style.

> I think in public life you take a position and I think particularly of the positions I've taken in the time I've been prime minister. I have to live with the consequences of those both now and into the future. And if I ever develop reservations, well, I hope I would have the grace to keep them to myself … You take a position and you've got to live by that and be judged by that – and that's my position.

At the heart of democracy is a contest of conversations. The tone of a democracy is set by the dialogue between a nation and its leaders. For the last decade, Australia has had a prime minister who thinks it beneath him to admit mistakes. Speers could hardly believe his ears: "He was virtually saying, even if I think I'm wrong, I'm not going to tell you." In one of the few press commentaries on this extraordinary moment, my colleague Peter Hartcher wrote of Howard putting himself "beyond political resolve into a realm of almost superhuman recalcitrance."

Debate ploughs on in Australia. Hansard is fatter than ever. The Prime Minister is always at the microphone. But after being belittled for most of his political career, Howard came to power determined public debate would be conducted on his terms. They are subtle, bizarre and at times brutal. This essay is about those terms and why Australians put up with them. Since 1996, Howard has cowed his critics, muffled the press, intimidated the ABC, gagged scientists, silenced non-government organisations, neutered Canberra's mandarins, curtailed parliamentary scrutiny, censored the arts, banned books, criminalised protest and prosecuted whistleblowers.

This is not as Howard advertised himself on arrival. Then he spoke proudly of his party's tradition of defending individual liberty and the rule of law. He still does. He painted his victory as a repudiation of "stultifying political correctness" that left Australians able "to speak a little more freely and a little more openly about what they feel." The ravings of Pauline Hanson he represented as a triumph of free speech over stifling orthodoxy. And after Aboriginal protesters burnt the flag on Australia Day last year, he rejected calls for their prosecution. "Much in all as I despise what they did, I do not believe that it should be a criminal offence," he told Neil Mitchell of radio 3AW in Melbourne. "I do hold to the old Voltairean principle that I disagree with what he says but I will defend to the death his right to say it, and I see that kind of thing as just an expression, however offensive to the majority of the community, an expression of political opinion."

The Old Voltairean has fallen a bit short. He leads a government notably uncomfortable with freewheeling debate. Uncomfortable is too kind a description: the dislike is profound. For a decade now, public debate has been bullied and starved as if this were an ordinary function of government. It's important not to exaggerate the result. Suppression is not systematic. There are no gulags for dissidents under Howard. We reserve them for refugees. The occasional victories liberty wins in Canberra are illuminating. There are limits. But Howard's government has been the most unscrupulous corrupter of public debate in Australia since the Cold War's worst days back in the 1950s.

We haven't been hoodwinked. Each step along the way has been reported – perhaps not as thoroughly and passionately as it should have been, but we're not dealing in dark secrets here. We've known what's going on. If we cared, we didn't care enough to stop it. Boredom, indifference and fear have played a part in this. So does something about ourselves we rarely face: Australians trust authority. Not love, perhaps, but trust. It's bred in the bone. We call ourselves larrikins, but we leave our leaders to get on with it. Even the leaders we mock.

We've watched Howard spin, block, prevaricate, sidestep, confound and just keep talking come what may through any crisis. Words grind out of him unstoppably. He has a genius for ambiguity we've almost come to applaud, and most of the time he keeps himself just this side of deceit. But he also lies without shame. Howard invented the breakable or non-core promise – the first was to maintain ABC funding – five years before those children weren't thrown overboard. The truth is we've known he was a liar from the start – though we didn't know, until he said so in Ho Chi Minh City, that he sees denying the obvious as a virtue, as the act of a graceful leader. Howard can admit error, but it is extremely rare. Apologies are almost unknown. More than any law, any failure of the Opposition or individual act of bastardry over the last decade, what's done most to gag democracy in this country is the sense that debating John Howard is futile.

One response has been to turn away and wait for him to disappear in the belief that Australia will once again be what we remember it was: free, open, principled, fearless, fair etc. It wasn't. Most of what troubles us now about the state of public discourse began under Labor. Many of us complaining now did not complain loudly enough back then as Paul Keating bullied the press, the public service and the parliament. But Howard has come to dominate the country in ways Keating never could. To the task of projecting his voice across Australia, he brought all the ruthless professionalism that marks his government. Perhaps the man has now exhausted his welcome, but even when the Howard years are long gone, we will be left confronting the damage done and the difficult question of how we let this happen.

As I started writing this essay, I began to keep a diary of outrages. I thought one or two examples of government bullying would be good to throw into the rhetorical mix. But they kept coming week after week: attacks by Howard and his ministers on open and honest debate. They continue as we go to press. Quite unexpectedly the essay turned into a snapshot of a couple of months of free speech sabotaged in a country that seems to be showing signs at last – though this could just be the Pollyanna in me – of being worried about what's at stake.

## February

### 13 FEBRUARY: *Joe Hockey monsters Professor David Peetz*

Joe Hockey's office was caught on the hop when journalists began ringing about lunchtime. Usually the minister's people sniff out trouble like this much sooner. Up on the Gold Coast, ACTU secretary Greg Combet was using research by Professor David Peetz of Griffith University to attack the government's WorkChoices laws. Hockey's press secretary, James Chessell, responded to press gallery questions by sending out a dirt sheet:

> **Peetz**
> - In 2001 he undertook an academic study on the work of union offi-cials – sponsored by the ACTU
> - His CV lists his research interests as "union membership"
> - He has been reported as being a singer in a "trade union choir"
> - He writes poetry for the "Workers Online" web site, which is "the official organ" of Unions NSW, which describes him as its "resident bard." Some of these poems include such partisan and infantile material like:
> - "Slug a worker or two" (to the tune of "pick a pocket or two") – "Why should toffs break their backs, stupidly paying tax? … Better to slug a worker or two"

- "You're fired" (to the tune of "Rawhide") – "My hearts calculating, for Johnny will be waiting, be waiting when we tell him, 'you're fired'"
- "Downsized" (to the tune of "Downtown") – "Listen to the workers as they open their surprises; Carve notches on your desktop as the count of bodies rises"
- In the aftermath of September 11 2001 he wrote a rather tasteless poem entitled "The Terrorist," which was published on the *Sydney Morning Herald* web site on September 17. In a week in which the world was in shock and extending its sympathy to the victims of this atrocity, David Peetz was writing a poem which included a verse about a terrorist telling "the President": "Evil will be overcome by good, but sir, you see, I know you are the evil one, and good is on my side! You are the force of Satan – and that is why I died!"
- His CV says that prior to becoming an academic he "worked in Parliament House in Canberra"
- In October 1999 Gough Whitlam gave a speech where he thanked "the men and women who have worked with me." This included David Peetz.

Later in the afternoon, Hockey's office issued a "backgrounder" attacking Peetz's findings, plus on-the-record comments from the minister ramming home the message that this man was a union fruitcake:

> Peetz makes some wild claims based on selective and shifting assumptions. Much of his data is out of date. We are surprised anyone is taking seriously a man the unions' online newsletter once described as its "resident bard." Peetz has described employers as "toffs." He has worked with Gough Whitlam. He has described the President of the United States as "the force of Satan." He is not credible.

Ruthless attacks on experts have defined the Howard years. The rough rule of thumb is this: the more unpopular the policy, the more brutal the government's response to its critics. Bring independent authority to bear on the Iraq catastrophe (Andrew Wilkie) or global warming (Professor Graeme Pearman) or WorkChoices (Peetz) and experts can expect rough handling. Frontal attacks are conducted by Howard and his ministers; more feral operations are carried out by parliamentary brawlers like senators Eric Abetz and the departed Santo Santoro. Work too grubby for them is left to reliable columnists, their efforts facilitated by ministers' offices giving them any assistance they need. The rest of the press can only watch and wonder at the access, the interviews and leaked dossiers that come the way of these attack dogs.

Howard's problems with WorkChoices won't go away. Australians took the passing of the legislation with characteristic passivity. There was none of the violence that saw France abandon, at roughly the same time, modest plans to reform its own employment laws. But the voters haven't settled down with WorkChoices. We've learnt to live with so much unwelcome change under Howard – even the GST – but not this. By late last year, industrial relations had come to concern Australians far more than Iraq, national security and threats to the environment. Peter Beattie was helped across the line in Queensland, and Steve Bracks in Victoria, by WorkChoices. When Joe Hockey turned his guns on David Peetz, New South Wales was also facing an election and opinion polls there were showing more voters worried by industrial relations than by any other issue.

The Howard government had responded to this wave of public disapproval by cutting off the flow of information about WorkChoices. A few months after the new laws came into operation in March 2006, the Office of the Employment Advocate – a division of Hockey's department – published some striking analysis of the impact of the new laws: everyone in the sample had lost at least one key award condition. Half had lost overtime; half lost loadings for shift work; 60 per cent lost penalty rates;

40 per cent lost rest breaks. Powerful and informed public debate followed. The Employment Advocate then mysteriously declared his own figures misleading and has from that time issued no comparable statistics on the operations of the new regime.

Peetz's disturbing analysis – first delivered to a conference in New Zealand on Friday, 9 February – dropped into this vacuum. Using the latest figures from the Australian Bureau of Statistics and Hockey's own department, plus private surveys and media reports, Peetz concluded that WorkChoices was having no discernible impact on productivity while causing an accelerated loss of award conditions. He found women were especially disadvantaged. But his most remarkable finding was that under the new laws, wages were actually falling, even though the labour market was tighter than at any time for the past thirty years. "Normally," he said, "real wages should be booming in such circumstances."

On the Monday after Peetz delivered the paper in Auckland, his university put out a press release summarising the findings and he did a few radio interviews. He was surprised by the response: "I thought that what the research was saying was pretty self-evident to most people anyway, but in hindsight realised that this was probably the first time some academic rigour had been applied to it." But it was not until the following day that the story really took off, when Greg Combet praised the professor and damned the government in a speech to the national conference of the Australian Workers Union on 13 February. The press rang Hockey's office for comment and out came the dirt.

Talk to Hockey's press secretary, James Chessell, and he will tell you he spent hours slaving over Google to put that little dossier of abuse together. Journalists recall receiving it within minutes of ringing him for comment. After issuing the follow-up "backgrounder" later in the afternoon, the minister gave a number of aggressive radio interviews and by nightfall was claiming (falsely) that the ACTU had commissioned the WorkChoices research.

The press served Hockey's purposes well. Some journalists disdained the dirt. Most didn't. Peetz says no journalist queried any of the allegations with him before they were published on the morning of 14 February. One journalist defended himself to Peetz by saying the result was balanced. That's what the doctrine of balance has come to in Howard's Australia: someone criticises the government; a minister abuses them in return; the press reports both without checking either – and that's called balance.

Hockey's work was not yet done. In Question Time that afternoon he took a dorothy dixer and rammed the attack home.

> On 17 September 2001, six days after the terrible terrorist attack in New York, he wrote a poem which included a verse about a terrorist telling the President:
> "Yes, evil will be overcome by good, but Sir, you see
> I know you are the evil one, and good is on my side!"
> This is a terrorist telling the President of the United States that he is evil and that good is on the side of the terrorist. This is the independent expert. He goes on to say:
> "You are the force of Satan."

A few facts about David Peetz: he publishes in leading academic journals; writes opinion pieces for Brisbane's *Courier-Mail*; has been professor of industrial relations at Griffith for three years and was president of the Association of Industrial Relations Academics of Australia and New Zealand in 2005–06. After this stoush with Hockey, seventeen academics from the United States, Britain, New Zealand, Canada, Germany and Australia wrote to the *Australian Financial Review* vouching for the high regard in which Peetz is held by academics in his field and deplored "what has the appearance of being an attempt to silence an intellectual critic and stifle debate in Australia through unfounded attacks upon his academic integrity."

Hockey's dirt file was not all wrong. As a fresh young graduate, Peetz was hired as a research assistant by Gough Whitlam, who had, by this time, retired from parliament and taken up a post at the Australian National University. Peetz helped him for three years with speeches, articles and books. Hockey was also right to say Peetz had worked "in Parliament House in Canberra." For a couple of years post-Gough and before joining the Department of Industrial Relations – where he would spend a decade at senior levels – Peetz was a researcher in the Parliamentary Library doing work for politicians of all parties.

And, yes, Peetz has had dealings with the ACTU, though why this should cripple him as a commentator on industrial relations Hockey does not explain. Some years ago, Peetz gave expert evidence for the unions in a test case on redundancy pay. He believes his research survived cross-examination unscathed. His 2001 study of union officials was conducted with the ACTU as "industry partner," but most of the cash came from the Australian Research Council with the approval of the then minister for education, David Kemp. Peetz has had both business and government as industry partners in research projects.

At this point, the misrepresentations turn nasty. Peetz did sing in the Brisbane Combined Unions Choir, but hasn't since 2001. And he writes satirical songs, bush ballads and poetry. A few days after September 11, he sent Margo Kingston's *Sydney Morning Herald* web diary a rather unhappy ballad in which the President and the Terrorist have it out in the Oval Office.

> The President opened the door, and saw inside the room,
> A ghostly apparition, with face of blood and doom.
> 'Twas the Terrorist he looked upon, at first he could but stare,
> Then flew at him with fists enraged ... they merely sailed through
>     air.
> He picked himself up off the ground, and turned to face the
>     ghoul.
> "You murdered untold innocents! There's none have been so
>     cruel!"

In the slanging match that follows, the Terrorist denounces the President as "the evil one" and "the force of Satan," but there is not a single line that suggests Peetz is on the Terrorist's side. The political message of the relentless AABB rhymes is that by choosing war to revenge the September 11 attacks on the United States, the President was playing into the hands of the Terrorist:

> Pleased with his work, this ghoulish monster faded through a wall
> His whole game plan was playing out now, right before his eyes
> As he settled down and waited for the body count to rise.

Good analysis. Bad poetry. The ballad was first used against Peetz in 2005, when he and a number of academics questioned the economic benefits of abolishing unfair dismissal laws. With characteristic ferocity, Eric Abetz rose in the Senate not to rebut the figures but to throw a bucket of dirt at the Queensland academic: "A person who engages in moral equivocation about terrorism will have no compunction whatsoever about deliberately misrepresenting our modest workplace relations changes." Abetz warned the ABC not to use this man as a commentator: "The ABC does itself and the Australian people no service by presenting someone like David Peetz as a respected academic."

Peetz is a fighter. He appealed to the Senate's Committee of Privileges, and in December Hansard carried both his response to Abetz and the text of "The President and the Terrorist" in all its glory. "I will not be dissuaded from speaking on industrial relations matters in public," Peetz told the committee. "However, my deeper concern is for the impact that such attempts at character assassination have on discouraging informed debate in Australia today." It did no good. Fourteen months later, when his research next challenged Howard government policy, all the old dirt was thrown at him again.

Griffith University did not spring to his defence. But in the wake of these attacks, the vice-chancellor of the ANU assured his staff they would have his backing in similar controversies. Professor Ian Chubb's email to all academics counselled and warned: "Engaging in public debate can, in the worst cases, expose ANU staff members to various forms of harassment, including ad hominem attacks, questioning of their integrity, and threats to their research funding or even personal safety." But he assured them:

> Staff members can expect to be supported by the ANU. This does not necessarily imply endorsement of the particular views they have put forward, but means defending their right to speak as an ANU staff member in their areas of expertise, and support for the general notion that public debates need to be informed by academic expertise and conducted with due regard to factual analysis and scholarly interpretation.

Peetz is now somewhat damaged goods in the eyes of the press after all this rough handling. The ABC is cautious. Though PM ran with the Work-Choices story for two nights after Hockey's blow-up, Peetz was not interviewed. He had been warned some time earlier by an ABC journalist that the government's attacks had made him a bit too hot to handle. Writing in the *Sydney Morning Herald* about the pursuit of Peetz, Adele Horin accused Hockey of trying to "scare journalists away from using him as a credible source." Hockey is still at it. One evening in late March this year, the minister told listeners to radio 4BC in Brisbane: "He writes for the trade unions, he sings in the trade union choir; after September 11 he praised the terrorists as heroes; and I don't think he comes to this debate in any way unbiased. And I never appreciate his commentary on these issues, but I'm happy to deal with the facts."

22 FEBRUARY: *Peter Costello threatens animal rights campaigners with the full force of the law*
When the mighty fashion house of Abercrombie & Fitch decided to boycott Australian wool in October 2004, it was another victory for an American lobby group with deep pockets and showbiz support called People for the

Ethical Treatment of Animals. PETA's brilliantly executed demonstrations and advertising campaigns had already embarrassed a few leading fashion houses into abandoning the use of fur, leather and fleece. In 2004, PETA was campaigning against the Australian practice of mulesing: cutting skin from a sheep's bum to stop it being eaten alive by maggots. Mulesing is painful and effective. So are PETA's tactics.

While Australian diplomats were dispatched to plead with the rag trade, the graziers' peak body, Australian Wool Innovations (AWI), was hiring scientists and spin doctors to counter PETA's campaign. But something seemed to snap when Abercrombie & Fitch said no to fine merino wool. AWI decided to sue. The architect of this strategy was the grazier, former minister in the Howard government and chairman of AWI, Ian McLachlan. He went about it flamboyantly. When PETA's president, Ingrid Newkirk, was flown out to debate him on 60 Minutes, McLachlan had her served with a writ on air. It made great television. As a process server materialised on the set, McLachlan crowed: "We'll see you again."

The case was a controversial disaster from the word go. The wool industry split. Dissident graziers raged about lawyers' bills and asked how the Australian Trade Practices Act could be used to sue an American charity with no assets in this country, which has only been campaigning against mulesing outside Australia, and does so under the free speech protections of the US Constitution.

The Act has tough rules against boycotts. If animal liberationists block a road with burning cars to stop live sheep being shipped to Saudi Arabia, they can be sued by either the farmers or the Australian Competition and Consumer Commission (ACCC). But it's a mighty leap for AWI to turn the same "secondary boycott" provisions against campaigners who lobby customers by turning up at foreign fashion houses to screen revolting videos of sheep having their bums cut away. PETA may be rich and dotty, but it's out there in the marketplace of ideas putting a point of view.

City media have barely touched this story, but it's been a big deal in the bush for years — not least because all woolgrowers are compelled to pay for the litigation whether they like it or not because it's being funded from AWI's annual levy on wool sales. The dissidents claim $8 million has already been spent on lawyers. AWI puts the figure at "$2 million to $3 million on Australian lawyers" plus another $7 million to $8 million on lobbying. Complicating an already very messy case is the rising price of wool, which means that the 103 growers and three exporters who have been recruited to give the case some local grunt can't claim PETA is actually causing them any direct financial loss. Even if AWI clears all the legal hurdles and the court is convinced PETA must be punished, the damages claimed will be rather modest. Meanwhile, with Hollywood's almost bottomless pockets of cash to draw on, PETA is eagerly awaiting its chance to parade anti-mulesing scientists, veterinarians and animal activists in front of the Federal Court – and the world's press – when the case gets under way early next year. Six months have been set aside for the stoush.

So things were looking grim when Peter Costello came riding to the rescue of AWI and his old political ally, Ian McLachlan. On 22 February, the Treasurer put out a press release announcing changes to the Trade Practices Act "to protect farmers suffering under an attempted international boycott of Australian wool by a US-based animal rights group." The precise changes proposed had yet to be revealed by the time this essay went to press, but it is understood Costello intends adding to the ACCC's old power to prevent interference with production and supply a new power to prosecute lobbyists who try to persuade customers not to buy. Several attempts by the Howard government to stamp out ethical boycotts of this kind have previously been blocked by a hostile Senate. That's no longer a problem.

Town and country agree Costello's plans to punish PETA are a bit rich. "It's people expressing a point of view about the way animals are being treated," said Cameron Murphy of the NSW Council for Civil Liberties. "People should be free to debate these issues." Grazier Charles (Chick) Olsson told me: "There are fellas out here you might call rednecks" – he wouldn't – "but they agree you've got a right to express an opinion, no matter how ludicrous it is." And what about all those boycotts Australians have taken part in over the years? We've boycotted French goods when nuclear testing was resumed in the Pacific; tuna caught in nets that drown dolphins; and carpets made by child labour in India. This year the world is celebrating the second century of British laws banning the slave trade, its end hastened by a civilised boycott of sugar.

Free debate is not high on Costello's agenda. Indeed, as he sues Random House over trivial insults from his past, rages at Muslim hot-heads, denounces ABC "bias" and drives the campaign to strip cash from student politics, he makes Howard look a rather moderate figure. And it's not that he's a poor debater. Costello is superbly effective on his feet: sharp, funny and cruel. But he is a man who will take what advantage he can to win an argument. When he has the power, he uses it. When questioned about his plans for the Trade Practices Act, he denied the changes he proposed would restrict freedom of speech. "You can say what you like. You can be as ignorant as you like. There's no law that's going to stop ignorant commentary, but there will be a law which allows the ACCC to stand up for Australian farmers when they suffer from a boycott."

24 FEBRUARY: *the Classification Review Board bans Philip Nitschke's Peaceful Pill Handbook*
Overturning the Northern Territory's euthanasia laws was among Howard's first dramatic acts and a marker for much that lay ahead under the new government. The move was profoundly undemocratic: Australians endorse euthanasia overwhelmingly. But it was driven by Christian conservatives, backed by the Murdoch press, attended by fierce scare campaigns and made possible by drawing on deep support from within the Labor Party. That 1997 victory casts a long shadow still. The political demands of anti-euthanasia forces are considered almost irresistible. What they want banned is banned.

The barbiturate sleeping pill Nembutal was banned in 1998. "In countries where voluntary euthanasia is legal and any drug can be used, Nembutal remains the drug of choice," writes the euthanasia campaigner Philip Nitschke. "But in Australia, it is only available from veterinarians, who use it as an anaesthetic agent during surgery, and as a drug to euthanase pets." With legislative reform impossible in Australia, Nitschke began to search for what he called a "peaceful pill" that might be homemade from legally available ingredients and "replicate the painless, easeful death provided by a drug like Nembutal."

The years ticked by. Nitschke worked on various "deliverance" machines while anti-euthanasia vigilantes continued to circle. In 2002, Canberra banned both the import and export of the machines and any documents that counselled, instructed or incited people to use them. In 2005, parliament debated one of the most thuggish little pieces of legislation of the last decade: the Criminal Code Amendment (Suicide Related Material Offences) Bill, which would make it a crime to use the telephone, fax, radio, television, email, mobile phone or internet "for the purposes of counselling or inciting suicide, or promoting or providing instruction on a particular method of suicide."

Labor supported the Bill. Opposing it were law groups, civil libertarians and Electronic Frontiers Australia. Christian groups called for even tougher penalties. Nitschke railed:

> Let us be clear, this bill's main aim is to prevent rational adult Australians from using a carriage service [phone, fax, radio etc.] to access any type of information about their end of life options. It should be realised that the censoring of this type of information will only promote the shameful national statistic of death by hanging as the leading means of suicide in this country. That is unless you intend to ban also shoelaces, belts, sheets etc. ... to criminalise the use of the telephone used by so many of our elderly members to stay in touch with important end of life issues strikes at the very heart of a free society.

In the Senate, only the Greens and Democrats attacked the Bill. The Democrats' Brian Greig gave it both barrels:

> Simply by typing the words "How to kill yourself" into the Google search engine I was able to access more than 7,230,000 hits in 0.1 seconds. This includes the site "How to kill yourself using the inhalation of carbon monoxide gas," which comes complete with step-by-step pictures. This bill will not and cannot ban this site or the thousands of others like it. In other words, simply with the click of a mouse, any computer can and will be able to access tens of thousands of pages of information on the topic of voluntary euthanasia, suicide and methods of killing yourself.

Greig wouldn't have a bar of the hypocrisy of Labor and Coalition senators who claimed the crucial issue here was not releasing the old from pain but protecting vulnerable young men from suicide.

> I have long had an interest in youth suicide prevention, most particularly from the demographic of gay and lesbian youth. A shocking statistic is that up to one-third of all same-sex attracted youth, those who are lesbian or gay, questioning their sexuality or perceived to be homosexual, attempt or succeed at killing themselves. I repeat: one-third. Australian and international research has repeatedly shown that harassment, discrimination, intolerance and prejudice aimed at young people who are homosexual, or presumed to be so and victimised for it, are key reasons for youth suicide ...
>
> So I cannot let it pass without noting the bitter and cruel irony that many of the religious organisations which made submissions in support of this bill are also some of the most vehement opponents of civil and human rights for gay and lesbian people ... It sickens me that religious organisations which passionately support this bill because of their declared passion for preventing suicide in fact have blood on their hands.

When the law came into operation in January 2006, Australia became the only country on earth to have such prohibitions. Countries, such as China, seriously determined to control access to the internet, aren't concerned about suicide. And anything like the Australian prohibitions would fail in North America and Europe by breaching free speech protections. So, alone in the world, two Australians discussing suicide methods on the telephone can be bugged and fined up to $110,000.

The sky fell in on Democrat Sandra Kanck when she set out to show how "stupid" these prohibitions were by giving a speech in the South Australian upper house cataloguing in some detail common methods of suicide. She quoted figures provided by the Australian Bureau of Statistics; she identified Nembutal as the drug Nitschke used while euthanasia was still legal in the Northern Territory; and she counselled against hanging, shooting and jumping in front of trains. Kanck welcomed the confusion her efforts would cause:

> Newspapers will be able to cover the whole speech, but they will not be able to put it on their website. Anyone who reads it in Hansard will be able to copy and distribute it, but if it is put on our website (as I expect it will be) it will not be able to be copied by anybody or forwarded electronically. If they do, they can be breaking the law.

The Labor premier was apoplectic. Mike Rann denounced both speech and speaker extravagantly, declaring this the most grotesque abuse of parliamentary privilege he had ever witnessed. Labor explored the possibility of expelling Kanck from parliament. Next day – with the Adelaide press clubbing the woman about the head – the government considered censoring her speech altogether from Hansard. That plan failed, but parliament took the unprecedented step of not posting the speech in the online Hansard. "The most important thing we can do is stop this how-to-commit-suicide information being put out on the internet," said Rann. "It is doing damage not just here but around the world."

Kanck spent that morning sending copies of the speech by post – perfectly legally – to anyone who asked to read it. Nitschke's euthanasia foundation, Exit International, swiftly had the speech on its website for the world to read. Apart from the ABC, the press outside Adelaide paid scant attention to this kerfuffle. Rex Jory was almost the only commentator to defend the woman in her home town. Out of step with his own paper, the *Advertiser*, Jory declared he was appalled by what Kanck had done, but censoring her speech was worse: "If members cannot speak their minds, state their opinions, express their views in Parliament without the threat of being gagged and vilified, then democracy is diminished."

*The Peaceful Pill Handbook* was launched ten days later in Canada at the sixteenth biennial meeting of the World Federation of Right to Die Societies. Nitschke and campaigner Dr Fiona Stewart had deliberately drafted the handbook so as not to fall foul of Australian censorship laws that forbid giving "instruction" in matters of crime. There's a long discussion – and legal warnings – about making barbiturates and other drugs. But Neil Francis, vice-president of Exit's rival, Dying with Dignity Victoria, declared the book's title misleading because it was not a practical, do-it-yourself manual. "While it does discuss a variety of suicide methods, it does so in rather technical detail. I, a biochemist for ten years, would myself have a great deal of trouble successfully implementing many of them."

Forty-five copies of the book were seized by Customs at Brisbane airport from one of Exit's volunteers when she flew home from the Toronto conference. Though Customs authorities considered the book fell foul of the 2002 import–export regulations governing suicide materials, *The Peaceful Pill Handbook* could still be printed and sold in Australia. This was hurriedly arranged after the airport seizure, and Exit International approached the Office of Film and Literature Classification for a clearance. The OFLC decided in mid-December that the handbook could be sold, but only to adults. It was in the shops for Christmas.

Morals campaigns in this country advance by plugging every hole. Once the fundamental decision is accepted – in this case, overturning the

Northern Territory law – every act of censorship that follows is represented as merely tidying up and blocking loopholes. Euthanasia remains a crime in all jurisdictions; the borders are sealed; the internet is cleansed; phones are silenced; and Hansard is censored. When the OFLC allowed adults to buy and read *The Peaceful Pill Handbook*, pressure was immediately brought to bear on the Attorney-General, Philip Ruddock, to plug a gaping hole. He needed little persuasion. Early in the new year, Ruddock referred the book to the Review Board of the OFLC – a sort of high court of censorship – in order, he said, to resolve the "apparent anomaly" of *The Peaceful Pill Handbook* being a prohibited import yet legally available in bookshops.

When the Review Board met on 7 February, it was addressed by counsel for Nitschke, the Right to Life Association (NSW), the NSW Council for Civil Liberties, and the Commonwealth. A fortnight later, the board announced its unanimous decision to ban the handbook for "giving detailed, although flawed and incomplete instructions in the manufacture of a barbiturate." A majority of the board added two further grounds. First, that by telling readers how to purchase Nembutal over the counter in Mexico and bring it home to Australia, the handbook "instructs in the crimes of the possession and importation of barbiturates." And second, that recommending friends clean up after a suicide may be an offence "under Coroners legislation in all states and territories." So even without the home chemistry and tales of Nembutal smuggling, *The Peaceful Pill Handbook* was doomed.

A month later, on the tenth anniversary of the overthrow of the Northern Territory legislation, Nitschke and Stewart led a march in Canberra that ended with the burning of 150 copies of their book. A few hundred people turned out for the protest, but it didn't make the television news and was barely mentioned in newspapers. Standing by the bonfire, Nitschke declared: "What we are burning here [is] access to ideas, access to information." A few days later he announced a version of the handbook would soon be available on the net for $37. It will be illegal to download, he said. "But people will take that risk because they feel they won't be tracked down." Taking on Google Books will be a mighty challenge for Canberra, but there's no reason to think the government won't try. It's only another hole to plug. The OFLC told the *Age*: "This is now an enforcement matter."

26 FEBRUARY: *The Commonwealth continues to hide what Canberra knew about the 1975 Balibo killings*
The fighting had passed through the town when Channel Nine cameraman Brian Peters led his colleagues into the square to surrender. Captain Yunus Yosfiah was standing a few metres away. He gunned Peters down and ordered his men to fire on all the journalists. Some died on the spot. The rest were killed when they ran back to the shop where they had hidden during the invasion. Three of their bodies, dressed in Fretilin uniforms and propped behind machine-guns, were filmed by Indonesian journalists. Then the corpses of all five – Peters, 29, Malcolm Rennie, 28, Greg Shackleton, 27, Tony Stewart, 21, and Gary Cunningham, 27 – were burnt. An Indonesian message was intercepted that afternoon by the Defence Signals Directorate (DSD) listening post at Shoal Bay near Darwin. There's evidence a translation went straight to Canberra: "Five Australian journalists have been killed and all their corpses have been incinerated/burnt to a crisp."

The Whitlam government lied then – and subsequent governments have lied ever since – about Australia's knowledge of the invasion of East Timor as it was happening. The official story has always been that the journalists died in crossfire and that Canberra took days to discover and confirm their deaths. For over thirty years, questions have hung unanswered over these events. Could the journalists have been saved? Were they sacrificed? Is Canberra so anxious to appease Indonesia that it has never revealed what it knew then – and knows now – about the deaths of the Balibo Five?

The umpteenth inquiry into the deaths began in Sydney in early February this year. Unlike all those that had gone before, this was a judicial exercise: an open and independent inquest before a NSW deputy state coroner, Dorelle Pinch, with the power to demand documents and compel witnesses to appear and be cross-examined. She heard evidence – never before revealed – that Canberra was aware of the deaths on the day they happened, 16 October 1975. The Shoal Bay operative, an ex-navy linguist called Robin Dix, told Pinch the Indonesians had used the word "dibunuh," meaning to kill with deliberate intent. "I will never forget it," he said. "I remember it word for word."

The intercept swiftly reached the highest levels in Canberra. About an hour after it was sent to DSD headquarters in Melbourne, the phone rang at Shoal Bay. Dix says a caller from the Prime Minister's Department asked: "Is this report true?" He replied: "You are on an unsecure line. Goodbye." Dix heard nothing more. And then the intercept evaporated. Crown counsel Mark Tedeschi, QC, told the inquest the text of that intercept is not among the documents provided by DSD. Nor is a document sighted twenty years ago by another witness, who was working on Kim Beazley's departmental inquiry into the killings. According to that retired senior army intelligence officer, a DSD operative showed him a file of twenty or thirty intercepts, one of which recorded an Indonesian officer saying words to the effect: "We have dead Europeans. What do we do?" And the reply: "Burn them."

These are secrets from a long time ago finally coming to light. It didn't last. After three weeks, the inquest was closed to the public. On 26 February, lawyers, relatives, spectators and reporters turned up to find the court attendants and transcribers replaced by federal officials. Alan Robertson, SC, the senior counsel who frequently pops up in crises of this kind, handed the coroner sworn letters from DSD claiming it would damage the service's capabilities if its "methods and sources" were exposed to the public gaze. Counsel for the family of Brian Peters protested that electronic warfare had changed greatly since the invasion. "These events occurred over thirty years ago, and on the evidence already before the court there's been a thirty-year history of deceit and cover-up in relation to the true story of how the Balibo Five were killed." But the coroner accepted the government's plea for secrecy, and over the next few days most of the lawyers and all of the spectators were thrown out every time DSD witnesses discussed techniques of interception.

The claim that keeping 1975's secrets is necessary to protect the security of Australia in 2007 was mocked by Des Ball, the country's leading academic expert on signals intelligence. He told Hamish McDonald of the *Sydney Morning Herald* that it's more likely the spies are trying to conceal failures of their own. "They don't want the texts of the intercepts of October 14 and 15" – the crucial days before the invasion – "made public because they don't want to deal with other possible translations and interpretations to the ones DSD has given the Government."

The intelligence services have never been so generously funded. Since September 11, Canberra has been pouring money into DSD, the Australian Secret Intelligence Service, the intelligence wing of the Federal Police and ASIO. In the urgent work they're doing now, they're supposed to be politically neutral and highly professional. We're told the bad old ways uncovered in the intelligence reviews of the 1970s and 1980s have been abandoned. Except, it seems, the self-protective instinct for secrecy. Keeping DSD's musty old secrets under wraps means dashing hopes that this inquest would finally bring everything about the Balibo killings into the open. But the government is backing DSD. Shutting the doors of the Glebe court could not have happened without Canberra's consent.

In a single month, embarrassing old intelligence secrets are protected, a text that offends Christians and frightens politicians is banned, animal rights campaigners are threatened with the law, and an academic critic is shamelessly slandered to try to destroy his reputation. What these moves have in common is a lazy, brutal assertion of power at the expense of public debate. Instead of allowing us to make up our own minds, the government resorted to insult, threats and suppression. These incidents weren't secret. All were reported by the press, though briefly for the most part and with little sense of the ugly pattern they reveal. This was just another month in Howard's Australia.

We roll with it because we have come to expect his government to behave like this. We're habituated. Christian warriors fighting sex on the screen demand film censors serve brief terms for fear exposure to all that filth will "desensitise" them. After a decade, Australia is desensitised to John Howard. So why doesn't Labor rally the nation to fight Canberra's bullying in the name of free speech? Because the party's heart isn't in it and Australians have only the patchiest record of becoming passionate about great abstractions — even the greatest of them, liberty.

We've never fought to be free. Vinegar Hill was a convict breakout easily and brutally suppressed. The officers who overthrew Bligh spouted liberty to trade in rum. Shorn of the colour, Eureka was a bunch of miners who didn't want to pay tax. The great issue that drove self-government for the colonies was seizing control of land. We were as much a part of the British Empire after Federation as we were before. And each step away from Britain had to be forced on Australia until the great Mother of the nation finally turned her back on us and walked into Europe. Australia surprised itself by refusing to accept Menzies' tyrannical plans to ban the Communist Party. But only just. Referendums opposed by any of the big parties always lose, and usually heavily. Liberty was preserved in 1951 by 50,000 votes in a nation of millions. The barricades have rarely been manned since.

We aren't the larrikins of our imagination. Australians are an orderly people who love authority. We grumble instead of challenging it. We despise politicians. Belittling them as a class is a cover for our own passivity. We elect leaders much as we hire electricians: we may whinge about the job and haggle over the bill, but essentially we leave them to get on with their work. The historian John Hirst writes:

> Australians think of themselves as anti-authority. It is not true. Australians are suspicious of persons in authority, but towards impersonal authority they are very obedient. This is a country which for a long time closed its pubs at 6 p.m. and which pioneered the compulsory wearing of seatbelts in cars. Its people since 1924 have accepted the compulsion to vote. Its anti-smoking legislation is so tough that smoking is prohibited in its largest sporting stadium, the Melbourne Cricket Ground, though it is open to the skies.

Touring the new United States in 1831, Alexis de Tocqueville observed a "mature and calm" individualism he had never witnessed in Europe. But had he returned to France via New South Wales, de Tocqueville would not have found the same character developing here. Where the United States was building a new society by balancing individualism and the needs of a free community, we were getting on with the business of being a British society at the far end of the earth: deferential, businesslike and orderly. This is not all loss by any means. The benefits of living in such a peaceful and lawful country are profound. But even today Australians remain subjects more than citizens.

Many puzzles of this subtle country can be solved by remembering how British we remain. It's structural. We have – and have voted to keep – the Crown. Our courts are British down to the horsehair wigs. The ethic of government is shifting from Westminster to Washington, but the framework remains British. We have a British suspicion of open information. Freedom of Information legislation hasn't challenged an instinct for secrecy deep within government, justice and business. We were together in the rearguard of democracies opposing guarantees of citizens' rights, particularly American notions of free speech. With Britain now absorbed reluctantly into Europe's human-rights regime, Australia remains the last Western democracy left without any national bill of rights. Polls tell us we'd like to have one – but we're not particularly concerned. It's another struggle for liberty we're not busting to fight.

David Malouf has a wonderful notion that Australia and America were made such different places by the English we carried in our baggage. To America, settlers took a language of high abstraction:

> Passionately evangelical and utopian, deeply imbued with the religious fanaticism and radical violence of the time, this was the language of the Diggers, Levellers, English Separatists and other religious dissenters of the early seventeenth century who left England to found a new society that would be free, as they saw it, of authoritarian government by Church and Crown.

By the time Australia was colonised, the language had changed. What came with the First Fleet was the English of the Enlightenment:

> Sober, unemphatic, good-humoured; a very sociable and moderate language; modern in a way that even we would recognise, and supremely rational and down to earth.

That could almost be John Howard's portrait of himself: the leader uncomfortable with high principle who prefers to deal in practical solutions. Over the last decade, "practical" has become a key Howard word used to stop debate in its tracks. Try to explore the principles behind his politics, and more often than not his talk turns to practical options, initiatives, outcomes, consequences, points of view, guidance, solutions, partnerships and so on. Perhaps the most famous phrase he's uttered in office is "practical reconciliation" – his cover for shredding the notion that white Australia had particular moral obligations to Aborigines. Ask him why asylum seekers who arrive by plane aren't also thrown into detention and he replies: "The practical circumstances are different." Ask why he hasn't signed Kyoto and he replies: "What we need to do is embrace practical measures."

Australians find this deeply attractive. As Malouf recognised, we don't live in a country – and we don't use a language – that revels in abstractions. Liberty and Freedom are not subjects of continuing public debate. We hear nothing like the great arias sung by American politicians in praise of fundamental freedoms. Accepting the 2004 nomination, George W. Bush delivered a passionate tribute to "the transformational power of liberty":

> Like generations before us, we have a calling from beyond the stars to stand for freedom. This is the everlasting dream of America and tonight, in this place, that dream is renewed. Now we go forward grateful for our freedom, faithful to our cause, and confident in the future of the greatest nation on earth.

Nothing remotely like that rhetoric is employed – or abused – by Australian politicians, though when he is standing in the Rose Garden or a paddock at the President's ranch, Howard gives it a bit of a go. Alas it falls to earth.

> Australia and America are close friends because above all we have similar values. In the end, the thing that binds nations together more than anything else is the commonality of their values and we have a view of the world that puts freedom and individual liberty, a belief in market outcomes where appropriate, at the centre of the activities of both our nations.

John Howard is, in his own eyes, a champion of liberty leading a nation whose commitment to freedom is "on a par with or better than the other great democracies of the globe." In the innocent days before September 11, he fought for the freedom of small businesses to sack; the freedom of parents to send their kids to private schools; the freedom of stevedores to employ non-union labour; the freedom of unionists to vote against strikes; the freedom of students not to join university unions. The preamble he and the poet Les Murray drafted for the constitution in 1999 guaranteed nothing while declaring Australians "free to be proud of their country and heritage, free to realise themselves as individuals, and free to pursue their hopes and ideals."

Despite reiterated claims over the years that Australia and America are at one in their commitment to freedom, Howard remains a resolute opponent of the document that guarantees that liberty in the United States. Hitler's Germany and Stalin's Soviet Union prove his point that even the most "beautifully written" bills of rights can fail utterly. Even trying is dangerous. "I believe that if you try and institute a bill of rights, you run the danger of limiting, rather than expanding, freedoms," he told Jon Faine of ABC radio 774 in Melbourne. "All you'll do is open up yet another avenue for lawyers to make a lot of money being human-rights specialists and practitioners." But the three institutions Howard claims guarantee liberty in this country are three he has worked to curtail almost from the day he took office: parliament, the courts and "a strong free press."

On paper, no country's prime minister could be more devoted to press freedom. Howard declares he's an "uncompromising supporter" of the cause and opposed to "any kind of censorship." He says he believes that "if you have a strong, free, on occasion rambunctious … press which is willing to have a go and is not in any way intimidated by the political process, then you are far more likely to have a strong, robust, virile democracy than with a bill of rights."

Yet under Howard, the press has found itself misled, intimidated and starved of information. On coming to power, Howard set about making sure the tactics he had used so brilliantly to claw down his rivals would not be turned against his government. There would be minimal tolerance for dissent within the party, the government and the bureaucracy. The great leaker would stop the leaks. Senior bureaucrats who survived the purge of the first weeks were instructed to report all calls by journalists to the Prime Minister's press office. Stories were doled out as rewards. More than ever under Howard, the press would win access through favourable coverage. The new communications minister, Richard Alston, was soon lashing the ABC over budgets and bias. Journalists were locked out of stories – particularly those involving the military and refugees – in ways Americans would find inconceivable.

On Australia Day 2002, the Woomera detention centre was in turmoil, with inmates on hunger strikes rioting and sewing their lips. A large number of press stood about in the desert that night watching. When ABC journalist Natalie Larkins questioned a police direction to fall back 200 metres from the camp perimeter, she was arrested. Other journalists and photographers were threatened with arrest if they did not move. Sydney's *Daily Telegraph* condemned the police operation as "the latest and lowest example of Canberra's censorship. This pattern emerged during last year's federal election campaign ... the scenes at Woomera on Saturday night would not have been out of place in the countries from which the asylum seekers have fled." But the Prime Minister mocked the idea that these scenes contradicted his sweeping support for media liberty.

> I'm concerned the press have total freedom in this country and people who pretend that because of what happened in Woomera yesterday that there's some restriction on press freedom, there's some attempt being made by the Government to cover up what is occurring in detention centres, I mean that is just ridiculous.

By this time, the twin towers had come down and Howard was wrestling with a new kind of rhetoric – both tough and reassuring. "We should never sacrifice basic civil liberties in pursuit of terrorists," he told Australian journalists gathered in Washington in June 2002. "Equally, we should never squirm from enacting new and strong laws simply because they may unreasonably offend some people." He promised he would never overturn "fundamental" or "generic" rights, but it was never clear which rights these were. Once habeas corpus went in 2005 – arrest without charge and detention without trial – it was difficult to see what bedrock rights remained. As each piece of security legislation fell into place, Howard would claim: "We think we've got the balance right." Attempts to understand how he weighed the scales proved futile. Instead of explaining himself, Howard pleads for sympathy as he attempts to resolve, in these difficult times, the "eternal dilemma" between security and freedom. "We are a society that respects the right of people and encourages people to exercise their freedoms to the full. And free societies always find striking that balance difficult. But that doesn't absolve us of the obligation to defend the freedoms that make us different."

The result has been a steady attack on the liberty of the press that saw Australia plunge to thirty-fifth place, behind many former Soviet Bloc countries, in the latest Press Freedom Index compiled by Reporters sans Frontières. A dozen senior journalists in the Canberra press gallery confirmed the slide when they spoke to Helen Ester for the collection of essays *Silencing Dissent*. Ester wrote:

> The interviews highlighted issues such as control and surveillance, and paint a picture of cumulative deterioration in sources of political news and information, describing new layers of disempowerment, frustration and disinformation. Most of the interviewees noted that the Howard Government had ushered in a decade of unprecedented executive control over political communication.

The Paris watchdog, the Canberra press gallery, the Australian branch of the Commonwealth Press Union and the journalists' union, the Media Entertainment and Arts Alliance (MEAA), all concur: the government is squeezing public debate. As evidence, they most frequently cite four cases:

• The long pursuit of journalists Gerard McManus and Michael Harvey for refusing to divulge the source of a story which leaves them, as this essay goes to press, awaiting sentencing for contempt of court.

• The chilling effect of bans on reporting contained in federal anti-terrorism laws passed since 11 September 2001, particularly the five-year prison sentences for reporting the detention without trial of suspects and witnesses.

- Difficulties placed in the way of reporting on refugees and asylum seekers who reach Australia by boat.
- The failure of Freedom of Information laws, which the High Court last year confirmed gives federal ministers virtually a free hand to withhold documents from the public. Calls for reform of the FoI laws by the press, NGOs, lawyers' groups and the Commonwealth Ombudsman have all been ignored.

Each year for the last three years the MEAA has published a report on the state of press freedom in this country. "Attacks on the Australian press are often indirect, pervading the law and its application, and filtering down through the attitudes of government and bureaucracy," the union wrote in the latest report, *Official Spin: censorship and control of the Australian press 2007*. "An anti-disclosure culture prevails and is enforced by government and corporate attacks on the press. The media are increasingly managed and marginalised by public affairs personnel, their requests for information are refused and their professional obligations criminalised."

Governments have claimed since the beginning of time that the last thing they're doing is censoring. There's always some explanation for information withheld: security, morality, respectability, order, fair play, care for the vulnerable, the rights of business, the rights of government. It's the same list of excuses used all over the world. But for a supposedly larrikin people, Australians are easily persuaded and oddly blind to the violations of principle these excuses cover. In the new political correctness of the Howard years, Australians are never racists and Australia is always free.

Commentators fill op-ed pages arguing the opposite. More ink than ever has been spent in the last few years defending the nation's liberties. The recent slew of reports, books and articles on the state of freedom in this country is evidence of growing discontent. There's never a night when some decent bunch isn't gathered somewhere discussing the bill of rights we have to have. But the steady constriction of public debate under Howard has aroused no deep concern in Australia. Only the little parties will touch the issue. Labor's indifference is colossal. We've accepted this as we've accepted so much in the last decade: not with enthusiasm, but with resigned forbearance. Isn't it just what governments do?

*Early March*

1 4 MARCH: *A dawn sweep through Sydney to arrest G20 demonstrators*
Sunil Menon was woken before dawn by a powerful light shining through his window. He would discover it was attached to a camera videoing the raid, but in the first confused moments he was aware only of the light, "serious knocking" on the front door and a man yelling his name. Menon says that in less than a minute the door was kicked open and about ten police poured into the house. One identified himself as a member of the NSW counter-terrorism unit. Another was a man Menon often noticed hanging around demonstrations in dark glasses and cargo pants. "I was scared when I saw him." In front of his housemates gathered in the sitting room, Menon was handcuffed and shown a search warrant. "They told me it was to do with G20."

Between fifty and sixty police from NSW, Victorian and Federal squads were out before the sun came up that day, arresting five students in raids around Sydney. The scale of the operation can't be explained by the chaos of Melbourne's G20 demonstrations last year or the relentless campaign for revenge driven by News Ltd's Herald Sun. The police themselves allude to the real driver behind the raids: the conference of world leaders to be held in Sydney this September. One of the arrested students says he has been told several times by senior police: "If you guys turn up to APEC, we'll smash you."

Tall and black with an unmistakeable face, Menon, 25, works at Sydney University's Fisher Library. A few years ago he was at the centre of a little cause célèbre after being charged with helping an escapee asylum seeker reach New Zealand. Menon's prosecution attracted street demonstrations, pleas from civil liberties bodies and an email from Thomas Keneally. The case collapsed. In August 2005, a Sydney judge ordered the jury to acquit for lack of evidence. On the morning of the March raid Menon was taken to the Sydney Police Centre and charged with two counts of aggravated burglary – it's alleged he was among G20 demonstrators who occupied office foyers in Collins Street – and two counts of unlawful assembly.

Daniel Jones, a heavy sleeper, was woken in his parents' house in East Balmain by a policewoman tugging his toe. He faced two or three police in his bedroom – who introduced themselves by name and squad as he lay there – and found another dozen in the hallway outside. Among them were counter-terrorist police. Jones, 20, is an arts student at Sydney University with a face known to many sports fans. He was one of the stars – not quite the word – of the SBS reality show *Nerds FC* screened during the World Cup. The fight against voluntary student unionism (VSU) drew Jones into campus politics. He was issued with two traffic fines after one of the big anti-VSU rallies in Sydney. He is now the education officer of the university's Students' Representative Council. At the Sydney Police Centre he was charged with affray, criminal damage and riot.

Dan Robins was woken at his girlfriend's place at 6 a.m. by frantic housemates in Newtown ringing with the news: "The police are trashing the house and they're looking for you." Later they told him about being brought into the sitting room in their pyjamas and twelve police searching their rooms. "They videoed my punk t-shirts and all the political stickers on the back of my door," said Robins. "They spread out my documents and videoed them – things like blood tests, union memberships, all these newspaper cuttings. They did the same thing in all the rooms. My housemates were really shaken up." Robins, 23, went to a city police station and turned himself in. A fine-boned, restless kid, Robins has been demonstrating for years. He was a schoolboy among tens of thousands of protesters on Melbourne streets during the World Economic Forum at Crown Casino in 2000. He's demonstrated often since and never been in trouble with the police before. At the Sydney Police Centre he was charged with two counts of affray, two of riotous assembly, two of reckless conduct and one count of intentionally destroying property.

Ten police came for Tim Davis-Frank at his parents' house in the beach suburb of Bronte. "My father answered the door in the dark at 6 a.m. in his dressing gown." As they gathered in the kitchen, Davis-Frank noticed through the window "guys in dark clothing and gloves sneaking around the back of the house to cut off any possible escape." He knew one of the squad: a Melbourne detective who had interviewed and released him on the evening of the G20 demonstration last November. Davis-Frank's parents explained their son was diabetic and he was allowed to eat a bowl of cereal before being taken to the Sydney Police Centre.

"This arrest is the second time I have experienced the force of Victorian counter-terrorism agents in relation to the G20 protest," wrote Davis-Frank in the *Green Left Weekly*.

> On the night of November 18, in Melbourne, I was snatched by about eight unidentifiable men and forced into an unmarked white van as I was walking with friends away from the protest. Without identifying themselves, the men in the van tied my hands behind my back, forced me to lie face down on the floor and proceeded to interrogate me, punching me repeatedly in the face if I didn't answer their questions quickly enough and once for accidentally calling one of them "mate."

Davis-Frank says he was taken to a Melbourne police station where the detective now standing in his kitchen arranged for his injuries to be photographed and told him he would be charged by summons for his part in the chaotic demonstrations that day. "The next thing I heard about it was four months later when they raided my parents' home."

Davis-Frank, 22, studies politics at Sydney University and comes from a political household. He says he was pushed in a pram to an anti-nuclear demo at the age of three months. "If you feel passionately about something, you should make your opinions known to other people," he explained. "Democracy should give space to express your voice. The more people who do, the richer society will be." At the police centre he was charged with two counts of aggravated burglary – those Melbourne office foyers again – three counts of riotous assembly and one of affray.

At the centre, the students saw a fifth suspect arrested in the early-morning raids: a seventeen-year-old high-school boy from Haberfield. He was leaning on the window of his holding cell: a distraught child on one side of the glass and his ashen-faced mother on the other. At some point in the day he was taken to the Children's Court, bailed and disappears from this narrative. The four remaining were taken after a few hours to the cells at Liverpool Central Court and strip-searched while they waited – most of the day – for the formalities of bail to be completed.

Honora Ryan was at Central Station early in the morning handing out anti-war leaflets to commuters when she heard about the arrests. She joined about thirty people gathered at the court to give the students moral support. A young piano teacher, Ryan was days away from graduating as a Bachelor of Music from Sydney University. She was not at G20, but opposition to the Iraq war had seen her demonstrating when Condoleezza Rice and Dick Cheney visited Sydney. She has never, she says, been violent at a demonstration. "I've shouted a lot. I go there and march and shout slogans. I'm a pacifist. I believe very strongly we shouldn't be violent – any of us."

The students didn't emerge from court until late in the afternoon. As they did, the Herald Sun was waiting. Their photograph would appear all over page one of Melbourne's Murdoch tabloid under a huge headline:

## COP THAT

The students dispersed and Ryan went down the hill to choir practice at Christ Church St Laurence, the Anglo-Catholic redoubt near Central. It was dark when rehearsal finished and Ryan emerged to find two big men in suits and dark glasses waiting for her. One held her elbow. They flashed badges. "When I asked to see them again, they wouldn't show me. They wouldn't tell me who they were." But they had a message. "They told me to stop going to rallies. They said they had a file like this on me" – she held her hands a couple of feet apart – "and to watch out or the same thing would happen to me." She took this to mean her house would be raided too. "I was really distressed. Nothing like this has happened to me before."

We don't demonstrate much these days. A million marched over bridges for reconciliation in 2000 – at which point the reconciliation movement died – and huge crowds turned out against the invasion of Iraq. The hard fact is that demonstrations in the last decade have stopped nothing in Australia. At best they've kept a handful of issues alive. Faith in the demo has collapsed – except perhaps when world leaders gather in exotic cities. The 1999 anti-WTO demonstrations in Seattle began a triple tradition of large turn-outs, occasional violence and heavy policing. Politicians are particularly gung-ho. National pride is engaged in keeping the streets orderly. After the World Economic Forum in Melbourne in 2000, Costello raged in private against the demonstrators. Bob Carr denounced the blockade of Crown Casino as "street-fighting fascism." Vietnam certainly knows how to meet the challenge: all the world's leaders gathered in Hanoi for APEC last year and there wasn't a demonstrator in sight.

Melbourne hosted the G20 meeting of economic leaders in the same weeks. The press predicted 20,000 demonstrators would turn out. Roads were barricaded around the Grand Hyatt in Collins Street. Police were bussed in from the suburbs. In the end the head-count was unimpressive – somewhere between 2,000 and 3,000. On Friday, 17 November, small groups briefly occupied about fourteen offices in the city. Some water damage was reported at the Australian Defence Force office. No arrests were made. The assistant commissioner of police, Gary Jamieson, described disruption in the city as "minimal."

Next day saw trouble. Early in the morning, about sixty protesters dressed in white anti-chemical suits burst through the barricades in Russell Street and headed for the Grand Hyatt chanting "our streets, our streets."

Their way was blocked by a line of mounted police. The *Age* reported the group, called Arterial Block, rushed the police lines a second time later in the morning but "dramatically dropped to the ground just a metre before the horses and started laughing. They then headed to join the main demonstration, a line of police horses following. There, they stripped out of their suits and masks and dispersed among the other protesters."

Who did what in the ugly afternoon that followed will eventually be decided by the courts. Newspapers reported "hit-and-run sorties" on police lines, a lone motorcycle cop being rescued by mounted police, the windows of an Isuzu riot van smashed with street signs, barricades pulled down, a television journalist assaulted, urine-filled balloons, wheelie bins, milk crates and other missiles thrown, the walls of a bank graffitied. Police were bitten, punched and kicked. A policeman sustained the most serious injury that day: a broken wrist. When the brawling had died down, Costello came out to the barricades to thank the police and condemn the demonstrators as thugs and criminals. "They organised themselves for violence, they prepared themselves for violence, they unleashed violence, they attacked property, they attacked the police, they tried to trash Australia's reputation."

Operation Salver was established within hours of the riot and began rounding up protesters. Police hunkered down to examine 10,000 photographs and 3,500 hours of footage, with the *Herald Sun* urging them forward. Next day, Drasko Boljevic was grabbed in a shop near RMIT University. "He was thrown into a white van by men who swore at him and failed to identify themselves," reported the *Age*. "He said he was tied up and one of them sat on his head as he was driven around the city. After being taken from the van near Flinders Street station, he was forced to kneel and was told he had been arrested." Detectives handcuffed him and took him to a police station. "I just think it's really bad what's been done to me," Boljevic said. "I just feel traumatised. I thought I was going to die because you don't know who these people are." He said he was 100 kilometres away in Malmsbury during the previous day's uproar. The chief commissioner of police, Christine Nixon, later confirmed that a man had been mistakenly arrested.

This democratic question is answered differently in every country: how much trouble do we allow demonstrators to cause? Even holding up traffic is verboten in Australia these days. As Dick Cheney's plane lumbered towards Sydney in late February, weighed down with armour-plated limousines, Howard, Kevin Rudd and the NSW premier, Morris Iemma, all insisted anti-war protesters had a democratic right to demonstrate against him – but they could not disrupt traffic. The prerogatives of the car are absolute except when they clash with the security needs of a world figure. While Sydney endured with good humour four days of traffic chaos necessary to keep Cheney safe – even the Bridge was closed to let him lunch with Howard at Kirribilli House – an attempt by a couple of hundred protesters to march a few blocks down George Street on the night of his arrival was met with the full force of the law.

In Town Hall Square Daniel Jones met old-timers who hadn't been on the streets since anti-Vietnam days. "It was a very broad rally. The Hicks issue had brought in a lot of small-l liberals." When the crowd voted to march to the US Consulate, he found himself in the front line. He claims that after arguing for the right of the demonstrators to move onto George Street, he was punched three times in the face, had his shirt ripped and was being held on the ground when a group of demonstrators dragged him back into the crowd. "I was basically beaten up."

For his part, Dan Robins claims he was dragged behind a police truck, held briefly on the ground, kicked in the groin and grabbed in a move known as the nipple cripple. He says a policeman repeatedly told him: "You've been identified as a wanted person." Wanted for what? The officer wouldn't say. According to Robins, he gave the officer some ID and was then told to clear out. One of the police added: "You're not allowed to be in the CBD today or tomorrow." Robins took the advice.

Early next morning Cheney was speaking at the Shangri-La Hotel in the Rocks. Barely 100 demonstrators turned out, but they included a former

Young Liberal with a banner that read: "The world needs more people like Dick Cheney. We love America." Sixty police standing shoulder to shoulder protected the hotel. A further fifty officers, including mounted police and dog handlers plus water cannon, were in reserve. All press reports concur that the gathering was uneventful until a move was made to arrest two members of the Tranny Cop Dance Troupe doing their usual street-theatre routine of mimicking police. In the mêlèe that followed, four arrests were made. The performers were charged with wearing police uniforms when not police officers. Pip Hinman, an organiser of the Stop the War Coalition, said: "It was quite clear to everybody else these young women were simply there as a bit of a gag."

But this is no time for jokes. Demonstrators are despised by the tabloid press and both sides of politics. Kevin Rudd called the old lefties and students who tried to march along George Street the night Dick Cheney came to town "a bunch of violent ferals and they should expect absolutely no sympathy." In the shadow of APEC, tempers are short. Police scrutiny is now part of the everyday life of universities. "They are so obvious," says Davis-Frank. "Old men in surf-brand Ts, three-quarter-length pants and running shoes." When rallies of any size are planned on Sydney University campus, security calls in the local Newtown police. When Senator Kerry Nettle addressed a meeting at Sydney University in March to discuss the US Studies Centre to be established on campus, two plain-clothes police joined university security to keep an eye on about forty students. Police deny the man taking close-up photographs of faces was one of theirs. The university, police and students consider such heavy policing absolutely routine.

The dawn raids in Sydney came a fortnight after Cheney's visit. Menon, Jones, Robins and Davis-Frank presented themselves to a Melbourne court the following week. The bail conditions of the twenty-eight Victorians charged require them to stay out of New South Wales. Going north to demonstrate at APEC will land them straight in gaol. Victoria seems to be planning a single monster trial of all the accused G20 protesters late next year.

17 MARCH: *Tamil asylum seekers are flown to Nauru after being held incommunicado on Christmas Island*

No one could get near them as they came ashore. The eighty-five men were brought in by barge from HMAS *Success* and herded onto Christmas Island's only wharf. The whole process took just over five hours. The islanders, who have long objected to the treatment given boat people on this distant speck of Australia, stood by the barricaded wharf holding sheets of cardboard reading "Welcome" and "Sri Lankans Ask for Asylum." That useful advice was also written on sheets hanging by the road the buses took on the ten-minute ride to the island's detention centre.

The new minister for immigration, Kevin Andrews, had told the press the bare minimum about the men, and he would do what he could in the weeks ahead to keep the record sparse. "I'm advised that there's been some suggestion that some of the people are seeking asylum." John Howard had already pledged that none would be allowed to reach the Australian mainland. He told listeners to radio 3AW in Melbourne: "It's an opportunity for Australia to send a signal to people-smugglers that they needn't think for a moment that our policy has changed."

The fundamental policy of Canberra from before the time of the *Tampa* has been to starve the public of details about boat people. They are to remain statistics – rather frightening statistics – not human beings with faces, stories, troubles and hopes. Labor began the policy. The Howard government made it famous with an order issued to naval photographers during the 2001 blockade of refugees: take "no personalising or humanising images." Keeping the press at bay has remained a top priority in all the operations that have followed to scoop up boat people wherever they appear and detain them on Christmas Island. One reason for spending nearly $400 million on the island's new detention centre is to keep the cost of investigating these stories very high. It's a long way to send reporters.

Only the *Australian* flew a crew to the island to meet the Sri Lankans: reporter Paige Taylor and photographer Andy Tyndall, an ex-London snapper who knew the island well. Shooed away from the camp the day after the men came ashore, they returned next morning via the shire rubbish tip and a patch of jungle to reach the back fence unobserved. Across a space of about thirty metres they were able to attract the attention of two men who were keen to speak. With their deadline approaching, Taylor and Tyndall retreated, sent a first report to the paper and returned through the dump and the jungle for more. They knew they wouldn't have another chance once that story hit the streets. By this time it was late afternoon.

"We fear for life," one of the men shouted through the wire. "We want to go to the motherland Australia." What would they like to say to the Prime Minister? "We want to stay in Australia, we want asylum, please." The men – they managed to speak to three in all – confirmed they were all Tamils fleeing the civil war in Sri Lanka. A place on the boat from Indonesia had cost them between US$5,000 and US$10,000 each. Why come here? "I like Australia – humanity." They were told of a boy called Gobi who had been let out of the camp, and on the next day Tyndall managed to snap his photograph. Though Taylor could not speak to him directly, she found out he was seventeen and had been on the move for a year after fleeing communal violence in Jaffna. Gobi was the single "humanising image" of these weeks: a face with a name and a few scraps of story.

According to the Australian government these people are not prisoners. They've committed no crimes. The legal pretence is that they're only held behind barbed wire for the convenience of processing. The rules say they are allowed to make contact with the outside world. But with only one or two lines into the Christmas Island camp, it isn't easy for asylum seekers to ring out, or anyone – families, support groups, lawyers or press – to ring in. A number of people have told me it proved impossible to reach the Tamils in the camp for nearly a fortnight after their arrival. Sometimes the calls rang out; sometimes they were answered, but no Tamil was brought to the phone. Some islanders say at times the lines seemed disconnected.

Information was almost as hard to come by in Canberra. A minor revolution had swept through the press section of the Immigration Department after the scandals over Cornelia Rau and Vivian Alvarez Solon. The place became more transparent, almost media-friendly. But the new minister, facing his first big challenge, was determined to take control of this story. The department's press office was gagged and only Andrews' office was allowed to make official comment on the Sri Lankans. His people claim the result was an efficient distribution of up-to-date information to the press. Journalists recall cooling their heels during these weeks waiting for not-very-useful answers to routine questions.

What news there was came out of Jakarta. The Indonesians weren't imposing an information blackout. They were happy to let it be known that Australia was trying to persuade them to take the Tamils back. And they were willing, but only on condition that the asylum seekers would then be returned immediately to the country – and the civil war – from which they'd fled. Such a breach of refugee norms was too brazen for Australia to contemplate. Negotiations continued for a fortnight. The foreign minister, Alexander Downer, was leading a new round of talks in Indonesia when five Australians were killed – and one journalist critically injured – in a plane crash in Yogyakarta. At this point the Australian government called it quits. Plan B was to negotiate with the bankrupt island state of Nauru.

The Dame Roma Mitchell Memorial Lunch on Friday, 9 March saw 320 lawyers gather at Zinc in Melbourne's Federation Square to hear two leading refugee lawyers, Claire O'Connor and Rebecca Gilsenan, discuss the impact of detention on the health of refugees. In question time, the refugee advocate Pamela Curr rose to ask the speakers what could be done about the predicament of the Sri Lankans. By this time they had effectively been held incommunicado on the island for a fortnight, unable to contact lawyers or, it seemed, relatives and Tamil community leaders in Australia. Curr also raised the plight of one of the men who had been brought to the mainland for medical treatment. Relatives living in

Australia – a doctor in Perth and a scientist in Canberra – had been refused contact with him by detention centre staff in Perth.

After a couple of forceful calls to the Immigration Department later that day, Curr was told there had been a "misunderstanding" and the asylum seekers would now be able to take calls. Wicki Wickiramasingham, chairman of Justice and Freedom for Ceylon Tamils, at last managed to speak to the men. "They were very afraid," he said. They told him they had been asking for asylum since the day the navy took them from the sea. But none had spoken to lawyers. They didn't know how; they didn't know any names; they were being told it was a very bad idea; there were language problems. "They didn't know anything." Wickiramasingham strongly urged the men to ask to speak to lawyers. But still it didn't happen.

The story of the Tamils on Christmas Island had died the death Canberra wanted. It sprung briefly back to life when Andrews announced that Nauru was indeed their next destination. On the afternoon of 16 March, the ABC's PM team managed to record a number of brief phone interviews with the Tamils. They pleaded to stay in Australia and be recognised as refugees. "We was arrested by the Sri Lankan Army and detained and tortured," said Sanje Selvanainar. "We was in the army camp over the forty-five days. Our five friends is shot in front of me." They spoke of torture, abduction, seeing friends murdered, their hatred of Tamil separatist forces – and of being denied access to lawyers by Australian officials. "We asked them," said Selvanainar. "But they didn't arrange."

The Immigration Department was playing its usual cat-and-mouse game: asylum seekers can only have a lawyer if they ask for one, and they have to ask for one by name. Holding them incommunicado for as long as possible is about denying them a voice in both the press and refugee processing. Good people take their careers in their hands to smuggle lawyers' names to asylum seekers. The minister responded to the accusations on PM that night by claiming the first request made for legal representation had come "in fact today." Two of the Tamils had spoken to Melbourne refugee lawyer David Manne that afternoon. Also that day a passionate plea by sixty-five of the men was faxed to the minister and given to the press. But it was all too late.

At 1 p.m. Christmas Island time next day, eighty-two Tamils guarded by sixty-eight immigration staff and Australian Federal Police were bussed to the airport and flown out aboard the last surviving passenger plane of Nauru's airline. No press were on hand to see them go. Messy though it was at times for the government, the operation had been a success: the men were out of the country before we came to know them.

Governments change. We don't. Not in any profound way. A radical government doesn't make us radical. A conservative government doesn't change our values. But when governments change, how we feel about ourselves and our country can shift a great deal. Howard came to power because a change in the nation's mood had already begun – a turning away from Keating's mantras of self-improvement – and the new man in Kirribilli House had plans to reshape the country's sense of itself fundamentally. On a long list of Howard's political achievements in the last decade, the mood shift of the nation is perhaps the greatest.

Wit disappeared. We're so acclimatised to the petty seriousness of the regime that we hardly notice any more that Howard hasn't come up with much memorably funny to say in a decade and has never – well, hardly ever – uttered even pithy remarks to skewer his opponents. Howard stands there insisting life and politics aren't funny. The great comic impersonators of Howard – from Max Gillies' one-man band to Terry Serio's devastating portrait in *Keating! The Musical* – make him a figure of fun but oddly unfunny. It's a strength: a nation that stops laughing at its leaders is more than ever under their thumb.

The bullying behind the calls for togetherness that powered his election victory in 1996 – slogan: "For All of Us" – is nakedly apparent now. Among the many things Howard has encouraged us to fear over the last decade – boat people, terrorists, euthanasia, unions, Islamic radicals, porn, drugs, black-armband historians, gay marriage, lefties, bird flu, interest rates under Labor, elites, chardonnay and residents who don't speak the lingo – we should add: each other. The defining mood of the Howard years is an uneasy fear of each other, the fear that we're growing apart, that we're not engaged in the same enterprise of being Australian.

Returning home in 1948 was a brave act for Patrick White. He was leaving Europe behind as Australian scholars, artists and writers fled there. Ten years later he wondered if he'd done the right thing. "Was there anything to prevent me packing my bag and leaving?" he asked in his famous essay "A Prodigal Son."

> Bitterly I had to admit, no. In all directions stretched the Great Australian Emptiness, in which the mind is the least of possessions, in which the rich man is the important man, in which the schoolmaster and the journalist rule what intellectual roost there is, in which beautiful youths and girls stare at life through blind blue eyes, in which human teeth fall like autumn leaves, the buttocks of cars grow hourly glassier, food means cake and steak, muscles prevail, and the march of material ugliness does not raise a quiver from the average nerves. It was the exaltation of the average that made me panic most …

Australia isn't what it was then, but the exaltation of the average is back in a big way. A great deal of effort by both the government and its outriders in the press has been devoted to mooring Australian public values in this thing they call the mainstream. Abuse of those who challenge mainstream ideas is routine in Howard's Australia. Even public commentators who pride themselves on their fearless independence routinely berate Australians for the sin of dissenting from the mainstream. It's a contradiction that should have us rolling in the aisles. Instead, this bullying has played its part in stifling debate in this country.

Mainstream was always an elastic term. When Howard rode to power promising to address "the real needs of the great mainstream of Australian society," he was talking about public debt reduction, mateship, support for small business and heterosexual families, and opposition to trade unions. Letting loose on race was mainstream, and when the time came, Howard would say he wasn't abolishing specialist programs of assistance for Aborigines, but "mainstreaming" them. While the course of this mighty river would shift over time, it always rolled over minorities. Delivering the Sir Robert Menzies Lecture in the year of his election, Howard concluded a long list of mainstream Australians with: "All those who do not want their national government to respond to the loudest clamour of the noisiest minority."

The word returned with a vengeance as Howard berated Muslims for not becoming true Australians. Around the world, the Right has enveloped justifiable concern about terrorism in a fantasy that Western values are under threat from Islam. An entertaining purveyor of this cultural panic, Canadian columnist Mark Steyn, was imported last year by Alexander Downer to deliver his big lecture "Does Western Civilisation Have a Future?" to enthusiastic think-tanks. Howard's version doesn't have the jokes, but does have the same theme: the danger Islam presents to Australia goes way beyond bombs. In Howard's nightmare of generalisations, "zealous multiculturalism" has exposed Australia to fragmentation and violence by undermining the reasonable demand that "all sections of the Australian community are fully integrated into the mainstream of our national life." He talks about decent things like democracy, the rule of law and respect for women. But he's also on about something more, something elusive, that involves silencing people who are out of step with Australian values. Howard wants the mufti Sheik Taj el Din al Hilali gone because he's "totally out of touch with mainstream Australian sentiment."

Nil doesn't begin to describe the chances of persuading Australians to accept sharia law. But early last year, there was a great outbreak of Australian values talk – led by Peter Costello – when a lone Muslim preacher claimed Muslims in Australia already lived under sharia law. Costello was right to correct Abu Bakar Benbrika: "There is not a separate stream of law derived from religious sources that competes with, or supplants, Australian law in governing our civil society." But Costello was in no mood to leave the issue to work itself out in debate. After whipping Benbrika's remarks up into an issue that somehow threatened the nation's survival, Costello delivered an ultimatum: the preacher should shut up or go. "If a person wants to live under sharia law, there are countries where they might feel at ease. But not Australia."

Howard is so much more subtle. He's impossible to pin down. He says the wrong things and the right things too. When Howard talks race, everyone hears what they want to hear. Simultaneously he keeps alive the vague and threatening notion that Muslims don't have the je ne sais quoi to be dependable Aussies. And he denounces bigots who attack the "main-stream of the Muslim community." (Yes, Muslims have a mainstream too.) And while he firmly rejects the idea that all cultures are equal, he offers a Howardian vision of multiculturalism in which "we want those other cultures to be part of our mainstream culture." Analysts call this "dog-whistling," as if Howard invented it. Old-timers recognise a man who speaks out of both sides of his mouth.

Howard's mainstream is not something pollsters can map. It's one of Howard's cleverest political inventions: his kind of people with his kind of values rebadged as the authentic voice of the nation. But here are a few items on a long list of Australian values Howard doesn't see floating down his mainstream:

- We're deeply suspicious of the United States. A couple of years ago the Lowy Institute discovered US foreign policy worries Australians as much as threats posed by Islamic fundamentalism. The institute confirmed earlier surveys which showed we believe strongly that the US has too much power and that Australia should steer its own path in world affairs.
- Nearly all of us believe the gap between rich and poor is too large.
- Support for invading Iraq without UN backing was in single figures.
- Despite a decade spent hammering the ABC for leftie bias, the government has failed to break the public's trust. Newspoll confirms the overwhelming approval of the nation, year in, year out. A Reader's Digest poll a few years ago rated the ABC the sixth most trusted government body, beating all the universities, the governor-general, the CSIRO and (in twenty-third place) Federal Parliament.
- We're not interested in worship. The last head-count had 9 per cent of us in church on any Sunday.

- We're rock-solid supporters of euthanasia, adult stem-cell research and a woman's right to abortion. On these issues, Cardinal Pell is totally out of touch with mainstream Australian sentiment.
- We believe business has too much power and goes unpunished when it breaks the law. Even before the latest changes, we were overwhelmingly convinced media ownership is too concentrated among a few rich families.

Complexity of this kind is unwelcome in Howard's world. After all he's a politician: they deal in simplifications while claiming always to have the people behind them. That's understood. Where Howard and his backers go too far is by insisting the same simple dichotomies – Them v. Us, Left v. Conservative, Minority v. Mainstream – should also be the underlying pattern of debate in this country. The notion that there's a "culture war" raging in Australia contains the same bleak idea that out there facing each other across no-man's-land are only two armies. Touted as a contest of values, this has actually been a party-political assault on Australia's liberal culture. In the name of "balance" between contending forces, the Liberal Party agenda has muscled its way into the intellectual life of the country. Of course it should be heard, but under these rules Canberra demands its agenda be taken seriously.

Meanwhile, the über-democrats of the Right are insisting we all live and think according to the will of the people. Among these democrats of the pen, none is more democratic than the Herald Sun's Andrew Bolt. Last November he drafted a magnificent indictment of artists out of step with the people and trapped in their "ghettos of hate": mockers of Bush and Howard (Peter Carey), makers of films about the stolen generations (Phillip Noyce), writers of plays about the slaughter of boat people (Hannie Rayson), novelists who demonise their country (Andrew McGahan and Richard Flanagan) and even pundits who crack jokes about wearing niqab (Phillip Adams). "But don't kid yourself that their contempt for mainstream Australia and its chosen politicians is unusual in their community. I'm afraid we're up against the group-think of the tribe."

I've got my doubts about one or two of the works he cites, but I don't want to see these artists punished for their anti-democratic tendencies. Bolt does. He argues it's high time Canberra stopped "the liberal use of taxpayers' money by the ABC, our universities, our research grant system and the Australia Council to fund attacks on our mainstream culture or institutions." He's not calling for anyone to be carted off to camps on the permafrost, but he does want to see anti-democratic artists suffer for being out of line. He is not alone out on the right in making these calls. What's surprising is that these not-uneducated men and women don't hear in their own words an echo of the rhetoric Moscow used to try to crush writers like Pasternak for being out of step with "the people who made the revolution".

Canberra has a taste for punishing dissent by cutting off funds. The Voltaireans of the Cabinet may be willing to sacrifice their lives for the sake of free speech in Australia, but they don't like paying for it. One of the grimmest sections of *Silencing Dissent* is the chapter written by its editors, Clive Hamilton and Sarah Maddison, analysing the fate of NGOs under Howard:

> In Australia, recent years have seen an unprecedented attack upon NGOs, most particularly upon those organisations that disagree with the current federal government's views and values. The attacks have come both from government itself and from close allies such as the Institute of Public Affairs. Questions have been raised about NGOs' representativeness, their accountability, their financing, their charitable status and their standing as policy advocates in a liberal democracy such as Australia.

Nearly 300 of the largest and best-known social justice, welfare, environment, disability, women's, family, youth and old people's NGOs took part in a survey conducted by the Hamilton and Maddison in 2004. They revealed a culture of threat in Canberra:

- The more government funding an NGO receives, the more constrained it feels in making public criticisms.
- Only a small minority of respondents believe that debates is encouraged by the federal government (9 per cent), with 58 per cent believing that debate is silenced and 33 per cent believing it is tolerated.
- 90 per cent of respondents believe that dissenting organisations risk having their funding cut.

There's nothing in writing. Threats are rarely made in so many words. As one NGO leader told the editors: "While not openly stated, it has been unequivocally conveyed that 'We do not fund organisations to criticise us.'" Those few words sum up the whole unhappy history of the ABC since Bob Hawke's time. Over the last twenty years, the impact on public debate of cuts and the fear of further cuts at the ABC is incalculable. The politicians mask their revenge behind a barrage of abuse about bias; the Howard government stacks the board with angry ideologues; and commercial news rivals print near-lunatic attacks. A personal favourite: Paul Gray birching ABC staff in the *Australian* last Christmas for their disqualifying failure to master "the basic outlines of Western metaphysical discourse: the tension between utopian political ideologies and the doctrine of original sin, for example."

For an irked minister in the Howard government, nothing is too petty. Alexander Downer flew to Jakarta in December 2005 to dispense hundreds of millions of dollars to clean up after the tsunami. No sooner had he left town than an apologetic embassy official turned up at the Jakarta International Film Festival to say that Australia was withdrawing its sponsorship of $18,000. The director, Orlow Seunke, was handed a letter from the Australia–Indonesia Institute – a division of the Department of Foreign Affairs and Trade – explaining the funding had been withdrawn because the Australian films selected for screening would not promote "greater mutual understanding between the people of Australia and Indonesia."

The festival was opening the next day. Seunke dashed off an angry protest: "You have put us in an impossible and very unfair situation." He never had a reply. But Seunke soon learnt that Downer had pulled the money because the festival was screening Curtis Levy's documentary *The President v. David Hicks.*

The Jakarta Film Festival is a ground on which the Indonesian intelligentsia meets the foreign communities of the city. It's a showcase for the cultural wings of the embassies – the British Council, the Goethe Institut, the Erasmus Centre etc. That Downer had pulled Australia's money at the last minute caused hilarity among diplomats and bemusement among Indonesians. After all those years preaching democratic values to Indonesia, an Australian minister had thrown a fit of pique in pure Suharto style. Owning up under questioning from Peter Garrett in April last year, Downer was quite unruffled.

Canberra has no coherent system of censorship by poverty. But there are enough outrages to keep everyone a little nervous, a little more circumspect than they might otherwise be. A video game called *Escape from Woomera* is attacked by Ruddock. *Through the Wire,* a verbatim piece about life in detention centres, gets no funding for a national tour from the then arts minister, Rod Kemp. Hannie Rayson's play that Andrew Bolt attacked – again and again and again – provoked senior ministers to call, behind the scenes, for the abolition of the Australia Council. Howard calmed them down, but Kemp reminded the chair of the Melbourne Theatre Company and chancellor of Melbourne University, Ian Reynard, that there are limits. "Why," he asked, "do you persist in biting the hand that feeds?"

A few years ago I was having coffee with a shrewd arts bureaucrat who had risen a long way and was planning to keep rising. No names. She wanted me to understand a maxim of the industry, something the hardheads kept in mind every time they went to Canberra begging for money. "If this government doesn't like something" – she meant politically – "you get nowhere pleading that we live in a democracy."

Late March

27 MARCH: *Allan Kessing found guilty of the decade's most embarrassing leak*
Within a week of the *Australian* publishing a leaked Customs report on the shambles at Mascot, Canberra had taken responsibility for security at all major airports and hired Sir John Wheeler to investigate the mess uncovered by the paper. After three months, the former chief of Britain's National Criminal Intelligence Service endorsed the leaked report, found that crime was flourishing at airports, security a sham and no one was in charge while bureaucrats fought endless turf wars. Wheeler found that when it came to "problems of deeply entrenched crime ... Sydney stands out in almost every category." Releasing the report in late September 2005, Howard pledged $200 million to address the problems.

As a squalid parallel to Wheeler's investigation, Australian Federal Police (AFP) were pursuing the bureaucrat who leaked the "highly protected" material to Martin Chulov and Jonathan Porter at the *Australian*. Police suspicion fell on Allan Kessing, one of the authors of the report, who had recently retired. A search of phone records revealed calls he had made to the paper's switchboard. On raiding his house in the Blue Mountains, police found a copy of the report plus a piece of paper on which Chulov's contact details were written. A raid on the Sydney house of Kessing's recently deceased mother netted Chulov's business card. Records of the pay phone down the street revealed that someone made a call from there to Chulov's mobile on the day before the *Australian* published the leak.

Kessing was charged under section 70(2) of the Crimes Act for communicating "without lawful authority or excuse" a document that had come into his possession while he was a public servant and which "it was his duty not to disclose." The penalty is imprisonment for up to two years.

Howard has been thrashing public servants – serving and retired – with the Crimes Act since he came to office. Nothing like this campaign to plug leaks has been seen in Australia in peacetime. While the public service drifts towards the Washington model of political control, Canberra has none of Washington's provisions to protect whistleblowers who go to the press. The secretary of the Prime Minister's Department, Dr Peter Shergold, called this sort of behaviour "democratic sabotage." Addressing the Australian Graduate School of Management in November 2004, he said: "Leaking blows apart the Westminster tradition of confidentiality upon which the provision of frank and fearless advice depends. So if some people seem surprised that I have called in the police to deal with leaks, they shouldn't be – I always have and I always will."

Only the week before, five Federal Police had turned up on the doorstep of the *National Indigenous Times*, a small paper published at a house in the Canberra suburb of Garran. The *Times* had just published news from deep inside Cabinet of dissension over Aboriginal policy. They had a warrant for two Cabinet submissions but left – after searching the office, house and car for two hours – with six. A number of public servants were grilled by Operation Furan over the leaks to the *Times*, but no charges were laid and no journalists were threatened with gaol. The raid was condemned by indigenous leaders, media heavies, civil libertarians, the journalists' union and the paper's editor, Chris Graham, who called the decision "mind-numbingly stupid or breathtakingly arrogant, or both."

For the AFP, this was the 113th investigation of leaks from the public service since 1997. By the following year, the number had grown to 120, on which the "leak squad" had spent 32,000 hours. Raids far outnumbered arrests, but the raids have sent a chill through Canberra. Several senior figures in the Canberra press gallery are on the record saying these are deliberately designed to intimidate the public service. "The impact of this goes far beyond access to the media," said Michelle Grattan of the *Age*. "They are intimidated generally, which has quite profound implications for policy." A few highlights from the work of the leak squad:

*February* 2003: Trent Smith, an official in the Department of Foreign Affairs and Trade, is stood down after Channel Nine reveals Downer telling the New Zealand High Commissioner that with or without UN backing, Australian troops would remain in the Gulf if war broke out with Iraq. A three-and-a-half year, $1 million investigation followed, with police sifting through 8,000 emails. Smith was cleared of the leak but eventually sacked in July 2006 for giving advice on Senate procedures to a member of Kevin Rudd's staff.

*June* 2003: Andrew Bolt of the *Herald Sun* publishes details from a highly classified report by Andrew Wilkie, who had left the Office of National Assessments to blow the whistle on dodgy intelligence used to justify the Iraq war. Howard's office had already spread the story that Wilkie was mentally unstable. Bolt mocked Wilkie's ONA predictions of civilian deaths and refugee numbers should war break out as "fairytale." (The figures proved conservative.) Downer's staff was widely assumed to be responsible for the leak, but no culprit was ever found. The *Canberra Times* reported "the observation of a senior policeman that anyone who could not solve this dastardly crime 'would not be able to find his bum with both hands.'"

*February* 2004: Michael Harvey and Gerard McManus of the *Herald Sun* embarrass the minister for veterans' affairs, Danna Vale, by showing how close she came to refusing $500 million in fresh benefits to war widows and former soldiers. The policy had been jettisoned before the paper hit the streets, but the AFP took the leak extremely seriously. After checking the records of 3,000 telephone extensions and hundreds of mobile phones inside the department, police arrested Desmond Patrick Kelly. Both Harvey and McManus – citing the journalists' code of ethics – refused to give evidence against him, and in February this year pleaded guilty to several counts of contempt of court. Meanwhile, Kelly's conviction has been overturned on appeal. He is home free, leaving the journalists to face gaol.

Allan Kessing is an abrasive kind of guy. Years ago he wrote scathing letters to the *Sydney Morning Herald* pointing out the stupidity – at various times and for various reasons – of the ABC, the Water Board, ID cards, gun control, logging, politicians grandstanding about cannabis, and voters who don't complete every box on ballot papers. In late 2003, he and Catarina Magni, his boss in the Customs Air Border Security team, finished their report on the shambles at airports: black holes in security and illegal activity by baggage handlers, air crew, ramp and trolley workers, security screeners and cleaners. The report was delivered, and nothing happened. But in the months that followed, airport security became a joke: first there was Schapelle Corby blaming everyone along the way for the dope in her luggage, and then David Cox looked out a window at Sydney airport and saw a baggage handler wearing his camel suit.

Kessing resigned from Customs the following month, May 2005, and three weeks later Martin Chulov and Jonathan Porter published their great scoop under the page-one headline "Airport staff 'smuggling drugs' – Secret Customs report exposes criminal links." Kessing has always denied being their source. But he was charged under the Crimes Act and made his first appearance in a Sydney court late in the year. As far as I can discover, Kessing's predicament went entirely unreported at this stage. The press was still focused on the last stages of the Harvey and McManus case.

Canberra does not lightly persecute journalists, particularly the usually friendly folks at News Ltd. But the impasse the government found itself in was entirely predictable: with no whistleblower laws to protect bureaucrats and no shield laws to protect journalists, this is where plugging leaks at all costs leads. Howard kept saying what decent guys Harvey and McManus were, and Philip Ruddock sent the Solicitor-General, David Bennett, SC, to court to beg the judge to drop the charges. This ham-fisted intervention didn't – and couldn't – work. Meanwhile, Ruddock talked vaguely about fresh laws to protect journalists, but nothing happened. Though caught in a bind, the government was showing no enthusiasm for dismantling the machinery of secrecy.

The case against Kessing was weak: phone records and scraps of paper. The only way to guarantee his conviction was to force the journalists to give evidence against him. For over a year after Kessing's first appearance in court, no demands were made on the journalists. Martin Chulov left the country to become the *Australian*'s correspondent in Jerusalem. It was only in early March this year, when the court case was about to start, that two AFP officers turned up in the foyer of News Ltd's Sydney headquarters with a subpoena for Jonathan Porter. The lawyers refused to accept it and the police left to stake out Porter's home address. After a couple of weeks they lost heart. In the course of Kessing's trial, it was revealed that the Commonwealth Director of Public Prosecutions had decided not to pursue the subpoena.

Kessing's jury deliberated for three days before convicting him on 27 March. *Crikey* declared this "a grim day for Australian journalism with a court verdict that effectively means public servants will have to be crazy brave just to take telephone calls from journalists." Curiously under-reported almost to the end, Kessing's case finally won some general press attention. The *Australian* attacked Canberra's hypocrisy: "As the Kessing case shows, the Government's professed support for journalists is meaningless while it continues to root out and punish whistleblowers who leak information in the public interest."

Harvey and McManus are waiting to be sentenced as this essay goes to press. On 13 April, Ruddock took a modest proposal for shield laws to his state colleagues in the Standing Committee of Attorneys-General. They offered no absolute protection for journalists who refuse to name sources, and no protection at all for whistleblowers who go to the press. The attorneys reject the proposal: some call for more protection. Some want none.

Howard's Ho Chi Minh City credo caused little fuss back home. David Speers filed his report with Sky News and waited for the story to break across the nation. It didn't. Some fine columns were written about the Prime Minister who makes a principle of not admitting mistakes, but editors and producers were generally unexcited by the news. Yet enough had been reported of that Park Hyatt press conference for the Prime Minister to want to claw his way back a little. A few days after his return to Australia, Howard told Neil Mitchell of radio 3AW in Melbourne that in saying leaders should never recant, he was really only criticising leaders who recant in old age. "If you're going to sort of change your view on these things, you ought to change your view on them while you are in office and while you've got some capacity to give effect to the change."

Mitchell seized the opening: "Well, do you look back on Iraq and say we've made some mistakes here?"

"I am still of the view that the decision we took three years ago, based on the evidence before us at the time, was right," Howard replied.

"Even though the evidence has proved wrong?"

"Well the intelligence didn't stand up, no. But Neil, when you are in a position of executive authority in a government, you have got to make a judgment on what you regard as the quality of the material before you ... Everybody said Iraq had weapons of mass destruction."

Mitchell persisted: "You're in office, look back, you got it wrong?" When Howard sidestepped the challenge, Mitchell came at him again: "Should we have gone in? In hindsight, should we have gone in?"

Howard wouldn't budge. "I do not retreat in any way from the decision that was taken."

Hard-heads would argue he has no choice here: for his own survival he has to spin, stonewall and deny the obvious disaster of the war. On one level, they are right. But on another — where truth matters more than political advantage — his performance shows how far debate in Australia has been corrupted by Iraq. And it's not just the war. As a dedicated ally of the United States, Howard locked himself and his government into a number of positions which could not then be usefully debated on this side of the world. Australia's views on terrorism, Iraq, Israel, rendition, global warming, torture and Guantánamo Bay were largely settled in the White House. If George W. Bush was, as he so famously claimed to be, "the decider," then Howard was left to be his distant echo.

"It was striking how much John Howard and Tony Blair sounded like Bush in the prelude to, and prosecution of, the war," wrote Peter Hartcher in the *Sydney Morning Herald* in April 2004. "It was no coincidence." He had discovered that an early-morning phone hook-up in Washington set the daily message for the Coalition of the Willing. On the line were Ari Fleischer of the White House, Pentagon spokeswoman Victoria Clarke, the State Department's Richard Boucher and two foreigners: one a Briton and the other a mid-level official of the Australian Embassy.

> The foreigners were there not to speak but to listen. The Americans would review developments overnight in Iraq, contemplate the day ahead in Washington, and devise a media strategy to best advance the agenda of their employer, George Bush.
>
> The Australian took notes of the session every morning, then relayed them immediately to Canberra, as the Briton would to London. The result was that ministers of the two junior allies had early and accurate access to the lines of the day from Spin Central and could speak as one. And they did. They created an Anglophone echo chamber on three continents.

Spin Central tells us the world we knew "changed forever" on 11 September 2001 and we must ditch many old ways to survive in this transformed existence. But of course, the world changes forever quite often. From the last hundred years alone I would nominate the Russian Revolution, the invention of television, splitting the atom, the Holocaust, the dissolution of the British Empire, the appearance of AIDS, the fall of the

Berlin Wall and the invention of the internet as world-changing events. But when Howard talks about the impact of September 11 – as he often does, particularly on big state occasions abroad – he deploys the rhetoric of a world transformed to justify the security machine he's put together piece by piece over the last six years to give us imprisonment without trial, home detention and fresh laws against talk.

Spin Central also says we must trust officials and politicians now in ways we haven't done before. To worry that ASIO or the police or Canberra bureaucrats might abuse their remarkable new powers denies the realities of a transformed world. Their mission is too serious to abuse. When Howard is questioned about the underlying principles of his new security apparatus, we have his guarantee that he can be trusted because he's got the balance right. How? He can't explain. The message is: trust me. But when the London bombings provoked another round of security legislation in the spring of 2005, a vanguard of sorts – lawyers, media proprietors, politicians on all sides, writers, film-makers, artists, citizens with long memories, citizens who know history – challenged Canberra's claim to be getting the balance right.

Howard needed all the premiers and chief ministers to sign up to these latest security measures. Nothing in the past decade so illuminates Howard's contempt for public debate as his wish that this happen behind closed doors. When the ACT Chief Minister, Jon Stanhope, put the latest draft security laws on his website, Howard was furious. Officials tried to drag them down again. The dramatic aura of secrecy surrounding the operation disappeared. The unwanted public debate that followed on preventative detention, control orders, shoot to kill and sedition was open, passionate and in many ways effective. Outrageous provisions disappeared and important safeguards were introduced into the legislation despite politicians and columnists denouncing the clandestine motives of the "civil liberties lobby".

Finding dark motives is the stock-in-trade of public debate under Howard. It's easy work. Slamming your opponent's motives means you don't have to grapple with facts; you don't have to answer arguments; you don't have to do any homework; and you can't be disproved. Articles, arguments, books and careers are dismissed for no more reason than the writer comes from the wrong side of the political tracks. I can't remember a time when party allegiance – real or imagined – counted for so much in public debate. While claiming to maintain perfect objectivity, Howard and his people blast away at the lefties, greenies, luvvies, unionists and Labor voters who can't be trusted and need not be listened to. A thumb-nail sketch of lies is all it takes to answer troublesome experts: David Peetz, the pro-terrorist union lover; Andrew Wilkie, the mentally unstable Greens candidate; Michael Kirby, the rent-boy cruiser of Darlinghurst.

Playing the man was nothing new in Australia – far from it – but in the Howard years it grew savage. Attack dogs inside and outside parliament prospered. From the worst of these people, John Howard carefully kept his distance. He was often a moderating public voice, urging calm when attacks on Muslims and Aborigines, for instance, got way out of hand. But with great skill he rode a culture of vilification that coarsened the public and intellectual life of the country.

In the spring of 2005, as Howard found himself under pressure to justify the severity of his security plans, the attack-dog columnists turned on the lawyers. Piers Akerman called them "rabid civil-rights and equal-opportunity dupes" in the *Sunday Telegraph*: "What is … apparent from the ravings of this coalition of the mindless is a mesmerising desire on their part to undermine the forces of law and order and erode authority, to the obvious detriment of the nation's well-being."

The lawyer Janet Albrechtsen, writing in the *Australian*, could see what really lay behind all that talk of human rights and ancient liberties:

> Look a little closer at these civil liberties groups, so readily quoted
> in the media, and it soon becomes apparent that these are a small
> band of activist lawyers with an agenda much like any other lobby

group. Even a cursory look at who they are, what they stand for and what they do reveals that "civil libertarian" is being used as a feel-good phrase, a smokescreen intended to hide political and personal agendas cunningly camouflaged as community welfare.

Who are they? Let's start with the NSW Council for Civil Liberties. Its website, which lists the executive committee and the general committee, includes former Labor candidates, former Democrat candidates, former Whitlamites, unionists, more unionists, recipients of union prizes, proteges of Labor academics. And so the list goes on. They are broadly representative of the community in the same way that, say, the Greens represent your average Australian. [Hold that thought.]

... there's nothing wrong with a bunch of leftist types publishing their preferred position on transsexual marriage, or speaking at conferences aimed at "Challenging the Neo-Liberal Danger" of the Howard Government, but let's not imagine that these people represent mainstream views.

They don't. Concern about the fundamental rules of democracy is not a mainstream worry. Most Australians take the ground rules of democracy for granted. Americans romanticise them. In 1939, Lincoln Cathedral's copy of Magna Carta – one of only four surviving – was the hit of the New York World Fair. Fourteen million people queued to see it, and when war broke out it was taken to safety at Fort Knox, where it nestled beside the American Constitution until the end of hostilities. The same copy of Magna Carta came to the Brisbane Expo of 1988 and caused no particular sensation. Queues were short and the cathedral was left with an embarrassing debt of £56,000.

But Philip Ruddock is a major fan. Asked by the *Weekend Australian Magazine* in January this year what event in history he would most like to have witnessed, Philip Ruddock nominated the signing of Magna Carta at Runnymede in 1215: "It probably has far more to do with democracy and the rule of law than any other event. Whatever else they say about me, I am committed to democracy and the rule of law."

Ruddock is one of the most fascinating figures Australian politics has thrown up for decades. He is a blank page in a dark suit. With power came a terrible seriousness and the face of a man who spends his time struggling with dark forces. For such an admirer of Magna Carta, his is a peculiar CV, for he has made his mark in two portfolios denying habeas corpus. Clause 39: "No man shall be taken or imprisoned or outlawed or exiled, or in any way destroyed ... except by the lawful judgment of his peers or by the law of the land." Doing just the opposite has been Ruddock's work for the government since 1996, from Woomera to Guantánamo Bay via Nauru. Yet he wears an Amnesty International badge as if it were a decoration for valour. Few credit him with that. Nor is there talk of a mighty intellect. Wit? No. Originality? No. Compassion? There have been times. Systems are his thing. Give him a system and he will apply it with shocking rigour. All holes will be plugged. His are more the instincts of a great bureaucrat than a minor minister. That makes him just the man for the job. Ruddock is the dark star of the Howard Cabinet.

As attorney-general, Ruddock is responsible for ASIO, the domestic intelligence service into which has been poured, since September 11, extraordinary fresh resources – money, personnel and legislative powers. Together with the Australian Federal Police, ASIO is aggressively shaping public debate in the name of the nation's security. Whether these actions are justified or not is difficult to assess. At the centre, there have been significant raids, big trials – with more on the way – and some convictions. Though new security rules make reporting these cases difficult, they appear to represent legitimate and successful operations. It's out on the fringes of ASIO's work that more immediate doubts arise, and it's out there that Ruddock is fighting to maintain absolute secrecy.

On a Saturday morning in September 2005, Scott Parkin was sitting in the Kaleidoscope Cafe in Melbourne when ten men arrived and took him to the local police station. An American political activist in his thirties,

Parkin had a track record for campaigning against Halliburton, the giant US oil-services company once run by Dick Cheney. The young American had been in Australia for a few months giving workshops in non-violent political activism. He'd also taken part in a few rallies. None involved him in violence. From the police station he rang a friend to say: "I've been told that a competent Australian authority has assessed that I am a national security risk." After being held in the cells for a few days, Parkin was thrown out of the country. There was no explanation, no charge, no trial and no chance to clear his name. Ruddock hinted darkly: "ASIO is responsible for protecting the Australian community from all forms of politically motivated violence, including violent protest activity."

Last November, the Federal Court granted Parkin's lawyers the right to see ASIO's assessment. That hasn't happened. The government was back in court immediately, claiming such a step could cause irreparable harm to national security. At least until the appeal is heard some time later this year, the lid stays firmly shut on the case.

Ruhal Ahmed never made it to Australia. He was one of three British boys who went out to Pakistan for a wedding in 2001 and ended up, after various wild adventures, in Guantánamo Bay. Their story had been turned into a prize-winning docudrama, *Road to Guantánamo,* by the fine British director Michael Winterbottom. Ahmed's tale had particular interest for Australians: for two years he lived in a cell close to David Hicks. "We couldn't see each other," he said. "But we could hear each other clearly, so every night for six months we spoke." The confessions forced from the three proved to be rubbish and the British demanded their release. The young men were never charged back home. Ahmed had travelled to Germany, France, Iceland, Turkey, Spain, Ireland, Holland and a number of other European countries to promote the film, but Australia refused him a visa "following a prejudicial security assessment by ASIO."

Now this episode becomes deeply bizarre. The Inspector General of Intelligence and Security was asked to investigate ASIO's role in the Ruhal Ahmed affair. He did so – and according to Ruddock's office he cleared the intelligence service. But neither Ruddock nor the inspector, Ian Carnell, will release a copy of the findings. Reading from notes which he believed were "very similar words" to those in the report, the minister's press secretary, Steve Ingram, said:

> The Inspector General of Intelligence and Security has completed his inquiry into the matter and concluded that ASIO acted legally and properly in making the assessment. They found the test was legally correct and the IGIS was of the view that the material available to ASIO was sufficient to conclude that this test was met, and went on to tell us that there is no indication whatsoever in the records that there was any political or external influence or attempt at such influence.

So the office of a minister who may have been accused of bringing improper political influence to bear can offer only a verbal assurance that the minister has been cleared. Ingram said: "Hope that is useful."

Last September, the Australian Law Reform Commission (ALRC) delivered its report on Ruddock's sedition legislation. This was the aspect of the 2005 security package that most directly challenged free speech, and these were the proposals that caused the most public uproar. If Australians are at last stirring about the fate of public debate in their country, it's largely because the Howard government has given fresh life to these ancient laws against political speech. The sedition provisions even gave the attack-dog columnists pause. When a handful of senators threatened to scuttle the legislation, Ruddock eased the bills through by promising an immediate review by the ALRC. The senators were duped.

In its report *Fighting Words*, the commission proposed thirty changes to draw "a bright line between freedom of expression – even when exercised in a challenging or unpopular manner – and the reach of the criminal law". To date, Ruddock has acted on none of them. He has ignored the recommendation that writers, journalists, performers, artists and academics be protected when going about their work in good faith. And he rejected out of hand the commission's fundamental suggestion that criminal penalties only apply to words *intended* to provoke violence. Just about every organisation of lawyers in the country backed the commission. They didn't want to see mere blather or angry commentary land people in jail. But Ruddock stuck to his guns: "The urging of the use of force and violence is, in its own right, dangerous and should be prohibited as a separate offence."

As I write this, I'm listening on the radio to the Prime Minister defending the "outstanding broadcaster" Alan Jones in the face of findings by the Australian Communications and Media Authority (ACMA) that in the week before the Cronulla riots of December 2005, Jones' words on air were "likely to encourage violence or brutality". Neither Howard nor the Labor leader now felt they should dissociate themselves from the guilty broadcaster. Kevin Rudd told ABC radio he had read nothing "which would cause me not to go on" Jones' show.

Not even this? By the Thursday before the riot, Jones was screaming like a race caller whose horse was coming home: "I'm the person that's led this charge here. Nobody wanted to know about North Cronulla, now it's gathered to this." He assured his listeners he "understood" why a text message was doing the rounds and read it on air five times: "Come to Cronulla this weekend to take revenge. This Sunday every Aussie in the Shire get down to North Cronulla to support the Leb and wog bashing day ..." Daily Jones cautioned his listeners not to take the law into their own hands, but he warmed to those who had exactly that in mind. Listeners' tales of vigilante action were read on air. This one he commended as a "good answer":

> My suggestion is to invite the biker gangs to be present at Cronulla
> Railway station when these Lebanese thugs arrive, the biker gangs
> have been much maligned but they do a lot of good things – it
> would be worth the price of admission to watch these cowards
> scurry back onto the train for the return trip to their lairs ...
> and wouldn't it be brilliant if the whole event was captured on TV
> cameras and featured on the evening news so that we, their parents,

family and friends can see who these bastards are … Australians old and new should not have to put up with this scum.

After considering the broadcasts for sixteen months, ACMA concluded Jones had caused his station, 2GB, to breach the Commercial Radio Australia Codes of Practice three times before the riot: once for encouraging violence and twice for broadcasting a program "likely to vilify people of Lebanese background and people of Middle-Eastern background on the basis of ethnicity." Despite his government putting into law the toughest sanctions we've ever had against fighting words, Howard was all praise for Jones in the aftermath of this decision. "I think Alan Jones is an outstanding broadcaster, I don't think he's a person who encourages prejudice in the Australian community, not for one moment, but he is a person who articulates what a lot of people think."

Somewhere out in the top paddock, a kelpie hears the whistle and turns towards his master. We've all heard this before from Howard: these racists are just saying what a lot of people think. A few years ago he was saying this in Pauline Hanson's favour: "I did understand that what she was endeavouring to articulate were concerns of some people who felt outside the political process." How perfectly it sums up the Old Voltairean who's sat atop public debate in this country for the last decade, that he sets the dogs on his critics, prosecutes bureaucrats, intimidates NGOs, rounds up street protesters, bans books, censors the phone lines, turns hardline Christian doctrine into law, undermines Freedom of Information, hides anti-terrorism operations behind punitive press laws and leaves dissenters exposed to sedition charges – but defends the prerogatives of racist rant, even when it edges over the line into violence.

April

13 APRIL: *Ruddock announces plans to ban all books, films and DVDs that "advocate" terrorism*

The curtain-raiser was an exclusive interview in that morning's *Daily*

*Telegraph.* "We are not going to allow material to be out there saying terror-ism is a good idea," Ruddock told Luke McIlveen. "This is a zero-tolerance approach to terrorism." The paper explained the problem:

> Under the existing Classification Act, material can only be removed
> from sale if it is deemed likely to "promote, incite or instruct in
> matters of crime or violence." The amended law – to be discussed
> at a meeting between Mr Ruddock and the state attorneys-general
> in Canberra today – makes it an offence to circulate material that
> "advocates" a terrorist act.

The paper deserved the scoop. *Telegraph* journalists have been trawling through Sydney's Islamic bookshops since the London bombings looking for scary material. The paper's "Secret Books of Hate" series in July 2005 provoked tabloid panic, police raids and the first promises by Ruddock to block any loopholes preventing "hate" books being banned: "I form a view they are sufficiently of concern that the law ought to be amended."

But the authorities turned out to be far less spooked than Ruddock and the *Daily Telegraph*. This would prove a pattern. The Office of Film and Lit-erature Classification looked at eight books and a film – presumably the worst of the material – and cleared them all for sale; the NSW police could find no reason to prosecute the bookshops; and the Commonwealth Direc-tor of Public Prosecutions found the books, pamphlets, DVDs and videos were neither seditious nor likely to incite violence. The *Tele* responded with fresh horror headlines:

### POLICE ALARM ON HATE BOOKS
*– Legal Loophole Puts Terror Manuals Back in Stores – Exclusive*

Ruddock was not defeated. He appealed, and on 10 July last year the Review Board banned two texts by the late Sheik Abdullah Azzam: *Defence of the Muslim Lands* "because it promotes and incites in matters of crime, spe-cifically terrorism," and *Join the Caravan* as "a real and genuine call to specific action by Muslims to fight for Allah and engage in acts of violence." The books are old – both were written during the Russian occupation of Afghanistan – and nothing in the worst passages of either would surprise anyone who has read newspaper accounts of suicide bombings in the last half-dozen years. These were the first books banned in Australia for decades. Melbourne University took the precautionary measure of removing them from library shelves. It remains the work of only a few seconds to download both from the internet.

Ruddock was not satisfied. He still wanted the rules changed to allow any text merely "advocating" terrorism to be banned. When submitting the idea to the state attorneys-general last July, he insisted: "We are not about curtailing freedom of speech." Rob Hulls, the attorney-general of Victoria, dismissed the proposal as "half-baked" and refused to back any immediate change. So did New South Wales. All last year, Ruddock continued to tout for their support while Commonwealth officials drafted discussion papers. Ruddock plans to ban any material indirectly counselling, indirectly instructing or directly praising terrorism – if such praise might inspire someone – however young and however mentally impaired – to commit a terrorist act.

That's throwing the net very wide. What is terrorism? If they are our friends, we call them partisans and freedom fighters. Only our enemies are terrorists. Would a flattering biography of the Israeli leader Menachem Begin – head of the militant Irgun that blew up the King David Hotel – be safe under Ruddock? What about a film that takes such a rosy view of the IRA that some young idiot might go out and shoot Protestants? And what do we do with all those glowing accounts by Reagan loyalists of the savage tactics of the Contras in Nicaragua? Then there's the problem of a censorship regime defined by the unknowable responses of the mentally impaired. Where on earth might this take us in the end?

The "advocacy" issue came roaring back to life in January this year when the *Telegraph* reported the broadcast of a documentary in the UK called *Undercover Mosque*:

Sydney's most influential radical Muslim cleric has been caught on film calling Jews pigs and urging children to die for Allah. Firebrand Sheik Feiz Mohammed, head of the Global Islamic Youth Centre in Liverpool, delivered the hateful rants on a collection of DVDs called the Death Series being sold here and overseas. ... Sheik Feiz says in the video: "We want to have children and offer them as soldiers defending Islam. Teach them this: There is nothing more beloved to me than wanting to die as a mujahid [holy warrior]. Put in their soft, tender hearts the zeal of jihad and a love of martyrdom."

Channel 4's documentary exposed Saudi financing of radical preachers in Britain. Hidden cameras filmed these holy men denouncing Jews, homosexuals, women, modern society, popular culture and secular law. Channel 4's strategy was to compel Islamic leaders to take action against these men by bringing the rubbish they preached into the light of day. Australia's response to the brief but starring role of former boxer and Medina-trained preacher Feiz Mohammed could not have been more different. Here there was a clamour for prosecution and bans. The DVDs from which these electrifying moments of Sheik Feiz were taken – *Signs of the Hour* and *The Grave* – were immediately condemned sight unseen by Kevin Rudd, Morris Iemma, Jewish leaders and Kevin Andrews standing in for Ruddock. Andrews announced a police investigation.

Once again, professional scrutiny of the Sydney-made DVDs – which have been around for about four years – undercut the panic. To date, police have laid no charges. The Office of Film and Literature Classification passed the videos for sale. I have seen both. I wish I lived in a world where there weren't such preachers – Christian or Muslim – but the bare bones of what Feiz Mohammed has to say are familiar from divinity periods at Sydney Church of England Grammar School. They drummed into us the glories of Christian sacrifice in the early church and the fate awaiting all unbelievers – including Jews – on the Day of Judgement. Our preachers didn't wear beards and skull-caps. Nor did they quote Arabic.

As Anglicans they politely masked the cruelty of their message. Not the sheik: sitting in front of an unseen little audience, he brings a horrible satisfaction to his work.

I think The Grave would fail Ruddock's "advocacy" test. Feiz is preaching martyrdom: "The most honourable death is to die for the cause of Islam." Like death from abdominal disease, he tells us, martyrdom takes the true believer straight to heaven. Perhaps the soldier martyrs he extols include terrorists, but terrorism is not praised. The rhetoric is both tub-thumping and vague. It ranges across centuries. Parents are not asked to send their children out on bombing missions tomorrow, but to prepare them for life as "courageous warriors" by teaching them riding, swimming, archery and love of jihad. This does not include suicide missions: "Islamically, you are not allowed to wish for death." He hammers the evils of sex, alcohol and fast cars. Men are reminded to pluck their pubic hair and wash swiftly: "You are not allowed to talk while you are showering." A minute of this was dynamite on Channel 4, but fifty minutes is barely endurable.

In classifying The Grave PG (parental guidance for children under fifteen) the OFLC brought to bear considerations ignored by the press and politicians: context, purpose, intended audience and the knowledge that out there are other religions with such unhappy teachings:

> While the theme of Sheik Feiz' lecture is death and dying, for the most part it consists of quotations from the scriptures and the use of allegories to illustrate his talk and emphasise his points. Within this context of a religious lecture, the impact of the classifiable elements is, for the most part, very mild and the lecture is not unlike the sermons of other religions.

Signs of the Hour is home free on the Ruddock test. This rambling account of the end of the world hasn't a whiff of terrorism about it. Instead we learn that Gog and Magog will be destroyed; Ethiopians with thin legs will come to dismantle the Kaaba in Mecca; and a creature variously called "the one-eyed liar" and "Satan" will destroy an army of unbelievers that includes ladies, ignorant Arabs and Jews. The few moments from this DVD used on Channel 4 show the sheik's frank pleasure at the fate awaiting Jews. Classifying *Signs of the Hour* PG, the OFLC noted:

> At approximately 42 minutes he refers to the Jews in the army of The One-eyed Liar as the "army of pigs", and that they will be buried. He makes further reference to the armies of the Anti-Christ which will appear at the end of Time, stating "behind me is a Jew, come kill him." The impact of this last statement is mitigated by the consideration that there are parallels within other religious belief systems which contend that on the final day of reckoning, the followers of false gods will not be saved. In this context, the impact of this theme is no greater than mild.

So that the public would not stumble on this material unawares, the distributors were instructed to put warnings on each DVD: "Religious Themes".

At this point in late February, there was an odd hiatus in the story. The distributors had been given the go-ahead, but no one else realised the controversial DVDs had been cleared — until mid-April when the *Sunday Telegraph* reported: PG RATING LETS KIDS WATCH ISLAMIC HATE FILM.

The news was gold for Ruddock. The "zero-tolerance" scoop he'd given Luke McIlveen a couple of days before hadn't intimidated the attorneys-general. All they had promised was to look at the issue of widening the censorship net when they next met in July. If Ruddock had appealed the DVD decision — as he'd appealed Nitschke's handbook and Sheik Abdullah Azzam's tracts — he would almost certainly have had the PG rating upped to M or even R, limiting their sale to adults. Instead, Ruddock used the OFLC's decision as a club to beat the attorneys about the head. Within hours of the *Sunday Telegraph* hitting the streets, he called a press conference to declare the rules were to blame: he had to be given fresh censorship powers: "Sheik Feiz Mohammed's sermon ... clearly in my view advocates the carrying out of acts which would be tantamount to terrorism."

The story caught fire once more. Channel Nine led its news that night with clips from the Channel 4 documentary; next morning, Ruddock had John Laws in a lather about the release of the DVDs; and the following day the *Sydney Morning Herald*'s Gerard Henderson drew pompous conclusions from the OFLC's verdict:

> The office's failure in this instance underlines the inability of many key players in Western democracies to respond to, or even under-stand, contemporary challenges. This is particularly evident within the civil liberties lobby.

When I quizzed Henderson, he admitted he hadn't seen the DVDs and said he didn't think he had to. Hardly any of the furious commentators had actually watched Sheik Feiz in action. Even the attorney-general was con-demning the DVDs sight unseen. His spokesman, Michael Pelly, told me: "AG has seen the reported comments and the television footage but not the DVDs." The nation's top lawyer hadn't assessed the evidence. That was bet-ter for his purposes: he was conducting a purely political campaign.

Yet exposure was doing its work. Feiz had retracted what he said about Jews. "That remark was made in the heat of the moment and I regret it," he told the *Australian*. "It was not something I should have said and is not something I believe." He also claimed he was not advocating violence: "The jihad I speak of is not one of violence. It is one of personal struggle against things like mischievousness, temptation and personal harm." The Muslim community distanced itself from the preacher, and spokesmen urged that he be prosecuted if, in fact, he had broken any laws. McIlveen reported: "It's important to make clear that Feiz has long been considered an extremist by sections of his own community." *Signs of the Hour*, never a big seller, was withdrawn from sale and the distributors confirmed to me that the DVD was being "edited" before being put back on the market.

Despite this, Ruddock is determined to change the rules. With New South Wales and Victoria still holding out – or they were as this essay went to press – Ruddock is threatening to collapse the national, co-operative censorship regime if that's what it takes to get his way: "If the States and Territories continue to resist, as they have done for more than a year, then I may be forced to go it alone and make this change to the Commonwealth's Classification Act."

Australian children are taught not to speak. It's a big part of our upbring-
ing, learning to shut up, to listen, to wait until we're spoken to. The lessons
aren't without their point, but somehow the habit of holding back has
been drilled into the character of the nation. When we were kids, we
accepted our parents telling us when we could open our mouths. Perhaps
at some obscure level we still think keeping quiet will do us good when
Canberra tells us what we can say, what we can know, when we can
speak. Limits other countries don't accept, we take for granted. It's part of
our deal with authority. There are no figures on this, but I'd guess that
among democracies we'd have the loneliest whistleblowers.

We've let what's happened, happen. That's why we're deluded if we
imagine Howard's departure will see freewheeling debate flourish across
the nation. Over the last shabby months – election years are always the
worst – Labor has made some decent noises. There's been lots of "we want
to see the details" and vague assurances have been given that "it wouldn't
be like that under us". But Howard's heavy intervention in public debate
has been looking for a while like the house style of government in this
country. We may be uneasy when bureaucrats are jailed, kids rounded up
at dawn by squads of police, and academics monstered for speaking truth
to power – but when are we going to grasp there's a pattern here?

The other day, Howard gave a self-consciously big speech about the
future of the nation: "It looks ahead to an Australia rising to the challenges
of the next decade and beyond – to an Australia within reach." It is a piti-
less homage to prosperity. Don't get me wrong: prosperity is good. More
than mass immigration, prosperity has transformed Australia from the
mean sectarian country of my childhood into an infinitely better place. But
surely there must be something more to look forward to than this:

> Ladies and Gentlemen, priorities do matter in politics. My govern-
> ment's number one priority is strong growth, greater prosperity

and wider opportunity. An Australia rising to new heights while preserving our great traditions of a fair go and pulling together in times of adversity, an Australia where people have more choice in their daily lives and a strong sense of social cohesion. I've never understood or accepted the argument of those who say that one detracts from the other. By raising families, by employing other Australians, by giving back to their community, Australians show every day how the two of them go together.

What we might do with this prosperity, Howard doesn't care to say. We'll just work and raise families and still be fighting terrorists in 2020: "For a country like Australia, there will be no holiday from history or from the long struggle against terrorism." The most professional politician of our lifetime, who knows this country like the back of his hand, speaks to us as if he were addressing the shareholders of a prosperous little business in a promising neighbourhood, "the Asia-Pacific region, a region that will be the cockpit of history in the twenty-first century."

Maybe he's right – we're just in business here, a corner shop surviving on the say-so of the big chains up the road. And we live by the ethic of the corner shop: hard work, long hours, dipping into the till. And there's no time for this malarky about debate, truth, good sense, calm and liberty. Those are luxuries for other folk in other countries. Not for us. Maybe later. Governments are for keeping the door open, wages down and the customers in order. Out the back is a mess but the shop is as neat as a pin. The Prime Minister is on the footpath in a starched white apron. We're open for business and that's what matters.

# SOURCES

2     "entrepreneurial flair": address to the Royal Melbourne Institute of Technology International University Vietnam Conferring Ceremony, Opera House, Ho Chi Minh City, 21 November 2006.

2     "forever linked": address to the Opening of BlueScope Steel Plant, Phu My, 21 November 2006.

2     "iterations": John Howard, address to Asialink Conversations Dinner, Ho Chi Minh City, 20 November 2006.

3     "wrong, terribly wrong": *New York Times*, 13 April 1995, p.7.

3     "beyond political resolve": Peter Hartcher, *Sydney Morning Herald*, 24 November 2006, p.13.

4     "stultifying political": address to the Australia–Asia Society, 8 May 1997.

4     "to speak": *Australian*, 25 September 1996, p.13.

4     "Much in all": *Australian*, 27 January 2006.

8     Opposition is steady at roughly 60%: ACNielsen/*Age* polls reported in the *Sydney Morning Herald*, 19 June 2006, p.2, and *Age*, 26 March 2007, p.1. Beating Iraq etc. as an issue: ACNielsen/*Age* poll, 16 October 2006 – IR was the most important issue for 17%, Iraq for 7%, national security for 5% and the environment for 10%. Sudden appearance in state elections: *Sydney Morning Herald* reporting an ACNielsen poll, 21 November 2006, p.1. Polling just before the NSW elections: ACNielsen in *Sydney Morning Herald*, 23 March 2007, p.1.

9     "real wages should be booming": *Sydney Morning Herald*, 14 February 2007, p.7.

9     David Peetz surprised by the response: interview with me, 28 March 2007.

10    Hockey in Question Time: Hansard, House of Representatives, 14 February 2007, p.88.

10    Academics vouch for Peetz: *Australian Financial Review*, 21 February 2007, p.52.

12    "Pleased with his work": for the full text see Senate Hansard, 6 December 2005, pp.59–60.

12    Abetz warned the ABC: Senate Hansard, 8 November 2005, p.28.

12    "I will not be dissuaded": Senate Hansard, 6 December 2005, p.61.

13    "Engaging in public debate": Crikey, 21 March 2007.

13    "scare journalists away": Horin, *Sydney Morning Herald*, 17 February 2007, p.33.

13    Hockey on radio 4BC, Brisbane: 28 March 2007, source: Media Monitors.

14    "We'll see you again": *60 Minutes*, 21 November 2004, <http://sixtyminutes. ninemsn.com.au/sixtyminutes/stories/2004_11_21/story_1287.asp>.

15    "AWI puts the figure": AWI spokeswoman Sally Davidson to me, 30 April 2007.

15    "It's people expressing a point of view": Cameron Murphy, AAP report, 23 February 2007.

15–16    "There are fellas out there": Charles Olsson to me, 26 March 2007.

16    "You can say what you like": *Sydney Morning Herald*, 23 February 2007, p.3.

17    "peaceful pill": *Sydney Morning Herald*, 19 March 2005, p.35.

17    "Canberra banned": Customs (Prohibited Imports) Regulations 1956 – Reg 3AA and Customs (Prohibited Exports) Amendment Regulations 2002 (No. 4).

17    "Let us be clear": Submissions to the Senate's Legal and Constitutional Affairs Committee inquiry into the bill at <http://www.aph.gov.au/senate/committee/legcon_ctte/suicide/submissions/sublist.htm>.

18    "Simply by typing the words": Brian Greig, Senate Hansard, 23 June 2005 p.240.

19    "Newspapers will be able": Sandra Kanck, Hansard, SA Legislative Council, 30 August 2006, pp.548–52, at p.548.

19    "The most important thing": *Advertiser*, 1 September 2006, p.6.

20    "If members cannot speak their minds": Rex Jory, *Advertiser*, 5 September 2006, p.20.

20    "While it does discuss a variety": Dying with Dignity Victoria, newsletter 137, February 2007, at <http://www.dwdv.org.au/newsletters/nl_137feb07.pdf>.

21    "to resolve the 'apparent anomaly'": Ruddock's announcement, press release, 12 January 2007.

21    "unanimous decision to ban the handbook": Review Board of the OFLC, press release, 24 February 2007. The detailed reasons for its decision had not been released when this essay went to press.

21    "Nitschke and Stewart led a march": brief reports appeared in *Canberra Times* and *Age*, 27 March 2007.

21    "What we are burning": *Age*, 27 March 2007, p.7.

21–22    "But people will": *Age*, 1 April 2007, p.10.

22    "Five Australian journalists": evidence of Robin Dix, *Sydney Morning Herald*, 1 March 2007, p.7.

23    "I will never forget it": evidence of Robin Dix, *Sydney Morning Herald*, 1 March 2007, p.7.

23    "Dix says a caller from the Prime Minister's Department": Evidence of Robin Dix, *Sydney Morning Herald*, 1 March 2007, p.7.

23    "We have dead Europeans": army intelligence operative, *Sydney Morning Herald*, 3 March 2007, p.32.

24    "They don't want the texts": *Sydney Morning Herald*, 27 February 2007, p.3.

26   "Australians think of themselves": John Hirst, *Sense & Nonsense in Australian History*, Black Inc., Melbourne, 2006, p.306.

27   "Passionately evangelical": David Malouf, *Made in England*, Quarterly Essay, Issue 12, Black Inc., Melbourne 2003. p.46.

28   "The practical circumstances": John Howard, press conference, 13 April 2006.

28   "embrace practical measures": John Howard on Sky News, 2 November 2006.

28   "Like generations before us": George W. Bush, *Washington Post*, 3 September 2004, p.A24.

28   "Australia and America are close friends": John Howard at Crawford, 3 May 2003.

28   "on a par with": John Howard to Kerry O'Brien, ABC *7:30 Report*, 30 August 2000.

29   "free to be proud": preamble for the constitution, *Age*, 24 March 1999, p.1.

29   "I believe that if you try and institute a bill of rights": John Howard to Jon Faine, ABC radio 774, Melbourne, 25 August 2000.

29   "uncompromising" and "any kind of censorship": John Howard, press conference, 14 October 1998.

29   "if you have": John Howard to Jon Faine, ABC radio 774, Melbourne, 25 August 2000.

30   "the latest and lowest example": *Daily Telegraph*, 28 January 2002, p.14.

30   "I'm concerned the press": John Howard, press conference, 28 January 2002.

30   "We should never sacrifice": John Howard to journalists in Washington, 9 June 2002.

30   "generic": John Howard to Paul Murray, radio 6PR, Perth, 30 July 2004.

31   "We think we've" and "eternal dilemma": John Howard to Neil Mitchell, radio 3AW, Melbourne, 3 May 2002.

31   "We are a society": John Howard, press conference, 8 July 2005.

31   "The interviews highlighted": *Silencing Dissent*, eds. Clive Hamilton and Sarah Maddison, Allen & Unwin, Crows Nest, 2007, p.112. Ester's survey was conducted in 2002–03.

31–32   "As evidence": the RSB report on Australia in full at <http://www.rsf.org/IMG/pdf/rapport_en_bd-4.pdf>; Press Union in AAP report at <http://www.news.com.au/perthnow/story/0,21498,21385811-948,00.html?from=public_rss>; MEAA in Amy Coopes et al., *Official Spin: Censorship and Control of the Australian Press 2007*, Redfern, NSW.

32   "Attacks on the Australian press": MEAA in *Official Spin*, p.24.

33   "I was scared": Sunil Menon, interview with me, 4 April 2007.

34    "The police are trashing": Dan Robins, interview with me, 5 April 2007.

35    "My father answered": Tim Davis-Frank, interview with me, 4 April 2007.

35    "On the night of November 18": Tim Davis-Frank, *Green Left Weekly*, 28 March 2007, p.9.

35    "The next thing": Tim Davis-Frank, interview with me, 4 April 2007.

36    "I've shouted a lot": Honora Ryan, interview with me, 4 April 2007.

37    "street-fighting fascism": *Australian*, 12 September 2000, p.1.

37    "minimal": *Age*, 18 November 2006, p.8.

38    "dramatically dropped": *Age*, 19 November 2006, p.1.

38    "They organised themselves for violence": *Age*, 20 November 2006, p.5. Other details: *Sunday Age*, 19 November 2006, p.1; *Sunday Herald Sun*, 19 November 2006, p.2; *Herald Sun*, 20 November 2006, p.1; and *Age*, 7 December 2006, p.3.

38    "He was thrown into a white van": *Age*, 20 November 2006, p.5.

39    "I was basically beaten up": Daniel Jones, interview with me, 5 April 2007.

39    "Dan Robins claims": interview with me, 5 April 2007.

40    "It was quite clear": *Daily Telegraph*, 24 February 2007, p.4.

40    "a bunch of violent ferals": *Daily Telegraph*, 24 February 2007, p.4

41    "I'm advised": Kevin Andrews, press conference, 23 February 2007.

41    "It's an opportunity": John Howard, *Herald Sun*, 24 February 2007, p.11.

41    "no personalising": Evidence of Brian Humphreys to the Senate's inquiry into A Certain Maritime Incident, transcript, pp.1151–52.

42    Exchanges with the detainees: *Australian*, 27–28 February 2007, p.1.

42    Gobi's story: *Australian*, 2 March 2007, p.1.

44    "They were very afraid": Wicki Wickiramasingham, interview with me, 13 April 2007.

44    "in fact today": Kevin Andrews on PM, 16 March 2007.

47    "A Prodigal Son": *Patrick White Speaks*, Jonathan Cape, London, 1990, p.15.

47    "the real needs": *Sydney Morning Herald*, 4 March 1996, p.13.

47    mainstreaming of ATSIC's programs, John Howard, press conference, 15 April 2004.

47–48  "All those who": John Howard, Menzies Lecture, *Australian*, 19 November 1996, p.13.

48    "zealous multiculturalism": John Howard, interview with Alan Jones, 2GB, 21 April 2004.

48    "all sections": John Howard, address to the National Press Club, 25 January 2006.

48    "totally out of touch": John Howard, interview with David Speers, Sky News, 26 March 2007.

48    "There is not a separate": the best account of Peter Costello's speech is in Piers Akerman's column, *Sunday Telegraph*, 26 February 2006, p.79.

49    "mainstream of the Muslim community": John Howard, interview with Neil Mitchell, radio 3AW, Melbourne, 27 October 2006.

49    "we want those other cultures": John Howard, interview with Neil Mitchell, radio 3AW, Melbourne, 24 February 2006.

49    "We're deeply suspicious": *Australia Speaks 2005: Public Opinion and Foreign Policy* confirming findings of the 2003 Australian Survey of Social Attitudes (AuSSA) that found 80% of us think Australia should steer its own path in world affairs and 73% of us think the US has too much power in world affairs.

49    "Nearly all of us": *Australia Speaks 2005*, AuSSA, 84% of us think the gap between rich and poor is too large.

49    "Support for invading Iraq": ACNielsen survey, *Age*, 18 January 2003, p.1, only 6% of us wanted Australia involved in an invasion that didn't have UN backing.

49    "Despite a decade": the latest in this series is *ABC Appreciation Survey – Summary Report*, Newspoll, 2006; *Reader's Digest*, June 2004. AuSSA found 65.8% of us have a lot or a great deal of confidence in the ABC.

49    "We're not interested in worship": Christian Research Association, Kew.

50    "We're rock-solid supporters": *Dying With Dignity*, Newspoll, February 2007. "Should doctors be allowed to provide a lethal dose": yes 80% and no 14%. Adult stem cell research: Stem Cell Information Kit, May 2006, Biotechnology Australia – support for adult stem cell research at 75%. Abortion: Katharine Betts, *Attitudes to Abortion in Australia 1972 to 2003*, "A woman should have the right to choose whether or not she has an abortion": 81% yes and 9% no. AuSSA found 60.4% of us have not much or no confidence in churches or religious institutions.

50    "We believe business": AuSSA, 59.6% think business should have less power; 80% think when businesses break the law they go unpunished; 78.8% think (in 2003) that media ownership is too concentrated among a few rich families.

50    "But don't kid yourself": Andrew Bolt, *Herald Sun*, 8 November 2006, p.21.

51    "the liberal use": Andrew Bolt, *Herald Sun*, 16 May 2002, p.19.

51    Pasternak: *Inside the Soviet Writers' Union*, I.B. Tauris, 1990, John Garrard and Carol Garrard, p.139.

51    "In Australia, recent years": *Silencing Dissent*, eds. Clive Hamilton and Sarah Maddison, Allen & Unwin, Crows Nest, 2007, p.82.

52    "The more government funding": *Silencing Dissent*, p.91.

| | |
|---|---|
| 52 | "Only a small minority": *Silencing Dissent*, p.93. |
| 52 | "90 per cent of respondents": *Silencing Dissent*, p.95. |
| 52 | "While not openly": *Silencing Dissent*, p.92. |
| 52 | "the basic outlines": *Australian*, 28 December 2006, p.8. |
| 52 | "The director, Orlow Seunke": documents provided to me by Seunke. |
| 53 | "Downer was quite unruffled": Hansard, House of Representatives, 11 May 2006, pp.174–5. |
| 53 | "Canberra has no coherent": a full account of these incidents can be found in my "Theatre Under Howard", the Philip Parsons Memorial Lecture, 9 October 2005. |
| 54 | "Within a week": the *Australian*'s reports appeared on 31 May 2005, p.1, and 1 June 2005, p.1. |
| 54 | "problems of": *An Independent Review of Airport Security and Policing for the Government of Australia*, September 2005, p.111. |
| 55 | "Only the week before": *Media Watch*, 15 November 2004; *Herald Sun*, 12 November 2004, p.17. |
| 55 | "mind-numbingly stupid": *Age*, 12 November 2004, p.9. |
| 55 | "113th investigation": *Australian Financial Review*, 19 November 2004, p.66. |
| 55 | "the following year": Hansard, 16 June 2005, p.39. |
| 55 | "The impact of this": Grattan in *Silencing Dissent*, eds. Clive Hamilton and Sarah Maddison, Allen & Unwin, Crows Nest, 2007, p.104. |
| 56 | "Smith was cleared": *Age*, 12 December 2006, p.1. |
| 56 | Bolt's column on Andrew Wilkie, *Herald Sun*, 23 June 2003. p.19. |
| 56 | "the observation": *Canberra Times*, 13 November 2004, Section B, p.11. |
| 56 | "Michael Harvey and Gerard McManus": a brief summary of the case: *Official Spin*, pp.8–9. |
| 58 | "a grim day": *Crikey*, 28 March 2007. |
| 58 | "As the Kessing case shows": *Australian*, 28 March 2007, p.15. |
| 59 | John Howard to Neil Mitchell, radio 3AW, Melbourne, 24 November 2006. |
| 60 | "The foreigners": Peter Hartcher, *Sydney Morning Herald*, 17 April 2004, p.41. |
| 62 | "What is ... apparent": Piers Akerman, *Sunday Telegraph*, 30 October 2005, p.93. |
| 62–63 | "Look a little closer": Janet Albrechtsen, *Australian*, 12 October 2005, p.14. |
| 63–64 | "It probably has far": Philip Ruddock, *Weekend Australian Magazine*, 27–28 January 2007, p.10. |
| 65 | "I've been told": *Sydney Morning Herald*, 17 September 2005, p.29. |
| 65 | "ASIO is responsible": *Herald Sun*, 13 September 2005, p.11. |
| 65 | "We couldn't see": *SBS Insight*, 20 February 2007. |

65      "following a prejudicial": *Sydney Morning Herald*, 28 October 2006, p.7.

66      "Hope that is useful": Steve Ingram, interview with me, 3 & 4 May 2007.

66      "a bright line": *Fighting Words: A Review of Sedition Laws in Australia*, ALRC Report 104, p.10; fault element in urging violence, recommendation 9–2.

67      "The urging of": Philip Ruddock, *Sydney Morning Herald*, 18 September 2006, p.4.

67      "outstanding broadcaster": John Howard, press conference, 11 April 2007.

67      "which would cause me": Kevin Rudd to Jon Faine, ABC radio 774, Melbourne, 11 April 2007.

67–68   "My suggestion is": *Sydney Morning Herald*, 13 December 2005, p.6, and ACMA Investigation report 1485, 11 April 2007 at <http://www.acma.gov.au/webwr/_assets/main/lib101068/2gb%20-%20report%201485.pdf>.

68      "I think Alan Jones": John Howard, press conference, 11 April 2007.

68      "I did understand": John Howard, interview with Neil Mitchell, radio 3AW, Melbourne, 22 August 2003.

69      "We are not going to allow": *Daily Telegraph*, 13 April 2007, p.3.

69      "Secret Books of Hate": *Daily Telegraph*, 18 July 2005, p.1.

69      "I form a view": *Daily Telegraph*, 20 July 2005, p.7.

69      "But the authorities": OFLC decision, press release, 23 December 2005.

69      NSW police and Commonwealth DPP clearing the material, plus horror headline, *Daily Telegraph*, 15 May 2006, p.1.

69      "Review Board banned two texts": <http://www.oflc.gov.au>.

70      "Ruddock was not satisfied": *Australian Financial Review*, 28 July 2006, p.19.

70      "We are not about": Rob Hulls, *Australian*, 29 July 2006, p.8.

70      that the definition of "advocates" would follow provisions in the Criminal Code: *Material That Advocates Terrorist Acts Discussion Paper*, 1 May 2007.

71      "Sydney's most influential": *Daily Telegraph*, 18 January 2007, p.1.

73      "OFLC had cleared the DVDs": OFLC report at <www.oflc.gov.au>.

73      "The news was gold": *Sunday Telegraph*, 15 April 2007, p.11.

74      "The office's failure": Gerard Henderson, *Sydney Morning Herald*, 16 April 2007, p.3.

74      Gerard Henderson, *Sydney Morning Herald* 17 April 2007, p.9.

74      "That remark": *Australian*, 19 January 2007, p.1.

74      "It's important": *Telegraph*, 19 January, p.27.

75      "If the States and Territories": Philip Ruddock, press release, 15 April 2007.

76–77   "Ladies and Gentleman": address to Queensland Media Club, Sofitel Hotel, Brisbane, 23 April 2007.

Bill Bowtell

Peter Hartcher's essay is as elegant and erudite as its author. Hartcher correctly believes that economic outcomes shape political ones. That is, the better the economic results across key indicators – employment, interest rates and inflation – the greater the certainty that any incumbent government will be returned at the polls. He must therefore adhere to James Carville's First Law of Politics: "It's the economy, stupid."

Applying the general rule to Australia in mid-2007, Hartcher assumes that strength of the Australian economy puts the outcome of the imminent federal election almost beyond question – that is, a fifth victory for the Liberal–National Coalition. Hartcher expects that Howard will stare down the Opposition and again pull victory from the looming jaws of electoral defeat, just as he did in 1998, 2001 and 2004. He believes that Howard understands better than any other Australian politician how to stimulate the two opposed lobes of the brain of Hartcher's bipolar Australia – Horne's Lucky Country and Renouf's Frightened Country.

Howard's skill is to know just how much pressure to apply to bring about the desired political outcome. First, he will attack the frightened country lobe by conjuring up the hideous terrors that will ensue if Rudd were to win. Then, the stern father will be replaced by forgiving Dad proffering the political equivalent of a Bex, a cup of tea and a good lie-down. Why risk Rudd when you can stick with the Devil you know?

The shape of the scare campaign is obvious. Rudd will be painted as a naive, inexperienced control freak, a myth-maker about his family history and assassin of the Anzac Day Dawn Service, unable to be entrusted with running a $1 trillion economy. His religiosity will become a signifier of hidden zealotry. Rudd will become a baby-faced axe murderer stalking every coal-industry job and town, doing the bidding of a cabal of effete Europeans and shadowy United Nations scientists.

In Hartcher's view, the combination of stellar economic figures and Howard's undoubted campaigning skills cannot but deliver what would be Howard's greatest, and probably last, victory.

Hartcher's analysis is powerful. It has history and commonsense on its side. The economy has apparently never been better. In addition to the blessed trinity of economic indices – inflation, unemployment and interest rates – consumer confidence is at record levels, the share market is at an all-time high, and, in April 2007, the Australian dollar soared through the US$0.80 cent barrier with ease.

As of April 2007 almost the entire Australian political class believes that Rudd simply cannot win the next election. The commentators and learned observers have determined to their satisfaction that a Rudd victory is theoretically impossible.

The only trouble is that the Australian people seem stubbornly disinclined to follow the script. The completely unforeseen sensation of the 2007 political season, at least for the first half of the year, has been that the better the economy has performed, the worse the Howard government has slumped in the polls. Rudd has established ascendancy over Howard as preferred prime minister.

Instead of seeing the lazy assumption fulfilled that the Liberal government would surf the economic wave to the shore, we are witnessing a real contest between the as-yet-irresistible political force of Rudd Labor and the long-time immovable object that is the Howard government. The clever money remains on the immovable object, but the political weakness of the Howard government has been exposed. At least for the time being, the link between economic and political outcomes seems to have been sundered.

The reasons why this has happened deserve consideration. There are at least three good non-economic reasons why the unthinkable may happen and the Australian people may vote to change the party of government for only the sixth time in sixty years.

These reasons are age, arrogance and values.

First, age. John Howard is old. He leads a tired and tiresome government. Any policy good that he might have achieved has now faded into history. Howard refused to retire after his 2004 victory to permit a generational change in leadership. Prime Minister Costello would have been, and may still be, a far more formidable challenger to Kevin Rudd than John Howard. While Howard's acolytes in his party and the press gallery remain in denial, the real story of the government's 2007 polling collapse is that the Australian people seem to have turned against Howard and wish him gone.

Second, arrogance. The longer any government remains in office, the greater it revels in the certainty of its own convictions. To a long-term government, each election victory is like rebooting a computer – the sins and omissions of the previous term are wiped away. But while governments absolve themselves of their transgressions, the electorate remembers. The sins of the past are not forgiven but accumulate like toxic heavy metals in shellfish. The Howard government bears a heavy burden of accumulated grievances stretching back to 1996 – the imposition of the GST, the rapid escalation of tax imposts, the cynical exploitation of the *Tampa* episode and children overboard, and the scandal of the AWB bribery of Saddam Hussein's regime. The people no longer extend to this government that most precious of all political gifts – the benefit of the doubt. The government has been led by the same troika of senior ministers for over a decade – Howard, Costello and Downer. Each of them is now subject to the law of diminishing returns – the more they appear, the less interest they generate.

Third, values. In the end, economic outcomes are not the only determinant of political outcomes. Values, culture and ideology are also significant factors in determining the shape and nature of our societies. Economic rationalists have kidded themselves that ideology is dead, that neo-liberal capitalism has triumphed and enjoys widespread popular approbation and support. But when neo-liberals talk about the economy, they talk about macro-economic indicators. They do not concern themselves with the social effects of their economic policies. Economists have this luxury, but politicians do not. The economy of the economists and the commentators is increasingly not the "felt economy" of the people and the voters.

Peter Hartcher is certainly correct that the economy will more or less determine the 2007 election outcome. It is just that the economy he contemplates is not the economy in which the great majority of Australians now find themselves.

No ordinary Australian believes that one hour of work a week constitutes a job, but this is how employment is measured by the statisticians. No ordinary Australian believes that the introduction of the GST made the tax system fairer or simpler, but this is the conventional wisdom of economists. No ordinary Australian believes that taxes and charges of all types should take up to half of an average income, but for a decade Canberra has gorged itself on the proceeds of bracket creep.

No ordinary Australian believes that young people should lose penalty rates in the interests of the "greater labour market flexibility" so adored by business leaders. No ordinary Australian believes that the sale of Qantas to "private equity" will greatly benefit the travelling public, reduce prices or improve services, yet this was nodded through by the Howard government. No ordinary Australian contemplated in 1996 that their children would incur large HECS debts as the price of pursuing tertiary education, yet in 2007 the price of some courses now exceeds $100,000.

In the eastern suburbs of Sydney and Melbourne, house prices and incomes have never been so high. But in the western suburbs, house prices are falling. Real household disposable incomes are being savagely squeezed by a lethal combination of rising interest rates and petrol prices, increased job insecurity, the abolition of penalty rates under WorkChoices, confiscatory rates of income and other taxation, and rapidly rising government taxes and charges for basic services and utilities. On top of all this, a crisis in water supply has emerged in every Australian city and with great ferocity in Brisbane and Melbourne.

The Australian people are now holding Howard to both his 1996 promise that he would make them "relaxed and comfortable" and his implicit 2004 promise that interest rates would not rise. (This was not, of course, the wording of the actual commitment, but it was certainly the "take home" message of Howard's 2004 campaign.)

The obvious message being conveyed in the opinion polls is that the Australian economy of 2007 has not made the Australian people either relaxed or comfortable. Each interest rate rise is, for them, a reminder of the broken promises of the Howard government – from the "never, ever" GST to the destruction of workplace security and the high real increase in income taxation. It is this "felt economy" that is shaping the political environment of 2007.

If the government is to overcome the burden of the "felt economy," it must offer new hope, a significant reduction in the squeeze on real household disposable incomes and the restoration of some degree of job security.

The 2007 opinion polls demonstrate that a broad and deep anti-government coalition has emerged. The sheer size of this coalition has astonished even the hard-heads in the Labor Party, although not, perhaps, Kevin Rudd. Under the pressure of the coming campaign, this coalition may splinter, but as of April 2007 it is composed of four main elements:

- disillusioned Howard battlers driven back to Labor by worsening economic conditions in the real economy;
- former Greens voters who refused to vote for Beazley in 2001 over *Tampa* or for Latham in 2004 but who have now shifted decisively to Rudd over climate change and the environment;
- Queensland voters delighted at the prospect of both a Queensland-based prime minister and treasurer;

- lastly, and most ominously for the government, hundreds of thousands of small-l liberal voters who have finally decided to abandon the most conservative government in Australian post-war history.

These small-l liberal voters have been dismayed by Howard's embrace of Bush's America, and in particular by the decision to invade Iraq and the abuses of human rights associated with the detention of David Hicks at Guantánamo Bay. They are aghast at Howard's rejection of the need to reduce greenhouse gas emissions, to sign up to Kyoto or to embrace the issue of climate change. They reject Howard's de facto alliance with hard-line religious sects and groups and his intolerance of social diversity and change. Simply put, they believe that Howard has gone "too far."

For nearly twenty years, Howard and his party allies have conducted a jihad against Liberal moderates. Howard succeeded in purging the party of its moderate wing and in bringing the Australian Democrats to ruination, but he made a grave error in believing that the community political base of small-l liberalism would also evaporate. It has not.

The shape of the coalition that at the next election might remove Howard and Howardism is now clear. As of April 2007, the polls indicate that a majority of the Australian people is at least willing to contemplate pocketing the largesse of economic good times and then obliterating a government that it considers to be out of time, and out of touch. That the Howard government should be in this position only months before an election is extraordinary. The stakes are now immense for both sides. If Howard remains as prime minister until the election, and then secures one last victory, he will have established his primacy in the Australian political pantheon. If he wins, the ideology of Howardism will be cemented in place.

But if he loses, Howardism itself goes with him. If Rudd Labor wins, the prospect of a re-organisation of the Australian Federation beckons – perhaps by referral of powers between Labor governments rather than by referendum. In these buoyant economic times, a decade or more of a Rudd Labor government seems inevitable.

Rudd's challenge is to consolidate the new coalition that has emerged to support him. Quite properly, the government will do everything that it can to rip apart the elements of this coalition, and to expose Kevin Rudd to both microscope and blowtorch. But it is hard to escape the conclusion that the great necromancer Howard has morphed into the Wizard of Oz, pulling lever after lever behind a tatty curtain, mystified why nothing seems to work as well as it once did.

Bill Bowtell

|

Peter van Onselen

As the fate of Gough Whitlam indicated, Australia's federalist institutions do not reward a "crash through or crash" style of leadership. Unlike in Britain and New Zealand, where powers of parliament allow a headier pace of reform, Australian leaders must either build consensus behind their policies (the tactic of the Hawke governments through the 1980s) or win multiple elections if they are to leave a legislative mark on the body politic. In keeping with this principle, there has in the Howard government been more continuity than change, both with the previous government and with the style, if not the substance, of earlier conservative governments. Only in Howard's fourth term has this balance shifted somewhat, the lure of a Senate majority being too much to hold in check Howard's ideological convictions on industrial relations. On this point Labor and the unions are already pouncing, and there is some evidence that the public is starting to listen.

John Howard's most important contribution as leader of the Liberal Party has been to adapt the party's longstanding political philosophy to the political circumstances of his own era. By the time he became prime minister, a good deal of economic liberalisation had taken place at state and federal level, as Peter Hartcher rightly points out. While seeking to continue this trend, Howard's greatest challenge, and in retrospect his greatest success, has been to position the Liberal Party as a party of both globalism and nationalism. He inherited a stronger economy than did the previous Labor government (an economy Howard had managed as treasurer from 1977 to 1983), but he was also left to deal with those sections of the electorate that felt left behind by decades of profound economic and social change. This has assisted Howard in playing on voters' fears of a return to the Labor Party.

It is also the reason why Kevin Rudd presents such a serious challenge to Howard. Rudd is a social conservative not unlike the Prime Minister, making him a very different proposition to previous modern Labor leaders at the federal level. In electing Rudd as leader in December last year, the Labor party room decided that as much as they hated Howard and everything he stood for, they were prepared to turn to a similar social conservative to see off the man who had become the sum of all their fears.

The rapid pace of economic and social change over the past thirty years has made social conservatism an attractive political platform. There is some irony in the fact that Howard, one of the strongest advocates of liberal economic reforms over the past two decades, has reaped the political benefits of the resulting sense of social insecurity. There is even more irony in the fact that one last go at significant liberal economic reform in the shape of WorkChoices might sink Howard when he is pitted against a socially conservative Labor leader not unlike himself.

John Howard attracts the votes of social conservatives because he shares their values. Derided by critics as the politics of fear, a theme picked up and run with by Hartcher, Howard's social conservatism was buttressed by twin events in the lead-up to the 2001 election. The arrival of MV *Tampa* in August and the terrorist attacks in the United States in September of that year allowed the incumbent to capitalise on the electorate's desire for security. However, where his opponents see dog whistles, wedge politics and unalloyed racism, Howard has in fact succeeded in bringing up to date the conservative vision of a unified nation that can rise above sectional interest.

Even so, the language used to promote this organic vision has been somewhat contradictory. The Coalition election slogan of 1996, "For All of Us," was at odds with Howard's repeated calls to "middle Australia," "the battlers" and the "frustrated mainstream." His rhetoric of national unity was, paradoxically, directed at a fraction of the electorate weary of perceived favouring of minority groups by the ALP.

It is in the area of social policy more than economic prosperity or national security that the Howard government has regularly been accused of pursuing "wedge politics." The label has an unacknowledged normative dimension — all issues are divisive; that's why we have politics. Hawke's introduction of Medicare, Keating's pursuit of constitutional reform, and the Howard government's restrictions on gun ownership were all very divisive but are not described as wedge politics, presumably because those who so liberally use the term approve of these policies and disapprove of the minorities opposing them.

Dismissing Howard's agenda as wedge politics fails to take into account the political philosophy behind it. Here the contrast in style and substance with Paul

Keating's nationalism and social policy, centred on what we might become rather than what we are, has been crucial. Howard has encouraged disdain for elite opinion on social issues (as though somehow the prime minister stands aside from the nation's elite), which he has characterised as overly negative about Australia's past and present. For those at the forefront of Keating's cultural bandwagon, Howard has been too much to bear. However, characterising him as a reactionary and an opportunist misses the coherence (and potential longevity) of his policies.

A substantial section of the Australian population was tempted by Hansonism to turn its back on the world. Howard's conservatism finds a place for this constituency, uncomfortable with the social and economic liberalism of the time. Yet, on a host of issues, Howard has sided with the elite against provincialism: guns, free trade, foreign interventionism and taxation reform, to name but a few. He has managed to bring a degree of consistency to his government's program with his emphasis on nationalism.

Howard's battler image is enhanced by what appears to be a polarity between elite and mass opinion on almost every political issue. He is always battling against either public opinion (GST and Iraq) or elite opinion (refugees and Aboriginal reconciliation) and has usually won respect from voters when he invariably prevailed. Howard's success as a conservative has been to underline the importance of the local and the familiar in a time of rapid social and economic change, much of which he outwardly welcomes. But it is important, too, to bear in mind his role in the consolidation of the economic reforms undertaken by the previous government that continue to make Australia a more dynamic and progressive polity. Howard would tell you WorkChoices is the newest piece in the puzzle.

For these reasons, Australia never entered an era of Howardism. Unlike Thatcherism or Reaganomics, or even Fraserism, the brand of conservatism adopted by the Liberal–National Coalition government elected in 1996 defies easy description (which perhaps explains why Rudd has found it easy to attack Howard for being out of step with Menzies). The present government, like its leader, has a mixture of conservative and liberal views. It has been his conservatism, however, that Howard has primarily relied upon and which has been rewarded with repeated electoral victories.

Now, facing off against Kevin Rudd, Howard has a problem. Rudd is a social conservative with a healthy streak of pragmatism running through his veins. He is every bit as media-conscious as the Prime Minister. Like Howard, Rudd is cautious and won't make the campaign mistakes that Latham did in 2004. Running against a long-term government trying to sell an unpopular and radical industrial relations policy will make Rudd's life much easier on the campaign trail – at the very least he should pick up a large number of seats. That is, so long as Labor's industrial relations spokeswoman, Julia Gillard, doesn't repeat her threat to business that it might get "injured" if it sides with the Howard government on WorkChoices. But Rudd needs to win sixteen to form a government: a tall order in the normal course of events. Where might they come from? Rudd is a Queenslander, and the Labor Party is well placed to pick up seats there, now that it is being led by a social conservative from Queensland. Currently Labor only holds six of twenty-nine seats in the northern state. With a good showing, it should be able to win six more. In South Australia, Labor should pick up Kingston, Makin and Wakefield; in Tasmania, Bass and Braddon. Such gains would leave Labor needing to win only five more seats across the rest of the nation (assuming no losses – no guarantee when looking to Western Australia). To secure the extra seats, Labor will be looking to outer western Sydney seats such as Lindsay and Macquarie, and to the marginal Northern Territory seat of Solomon. Victoria doesn't provide Labor with many opportunities. The Labor campaign team is confident it can pick up one or both of the WA seats of Stirling and Hasluck, but with a booming economy in the west neither is a certainty.

Given this, the election result may hang in the balance until late in the count. For those of us who enjoy election nights, that would be a welcome change from 2001 and 2004. But unless there is a clear move on, Rudd is more likely to fall just short of, than just over, the line. Incumbent governments have an enormous advantage at election time. Government advertising in the lead-up to election campaigns and the targeting of marginal seats with taxpayer-funded resources could see Howard hang on with less than 50 per cent of the two-party vote, as he did against Beazley in 1998.

The Australian public is very conservative when voting to retain or throw out a successful government. So long as voters don't think Howard's radicalism on industrial relations has overtaken his social conservatism, he should get to depart at a time of his choosing.

Peter van Onselen

## Andrew Charlton

Peter Hartcher tells us in his essay *Bipolar Nation* that Howard is playing the 2007 election like a shrewd game of bridge. Labor can put down as many policy aces as it likes between now and polling day, but if Howard wins in the end it will be because he holds all the trump cards.

Hartcher believes that economics and national security are the only issues that matter and that Howard's commanding lead in these two areas makes him odds-on for victory. Certainly these issues are important, but I suspect that Howard is more vulnerable, especially on economics, than many people believe. Understanding this vulnerability is the key to a Labor win.

Well before the declaration that "It's the economy, stupid," politicians knew the electoral potency of economics. Margaret Thatcher used to snooker her left-wing opponents by pointing out that progressive social policies are useless if they can't be financed, once famously using a biblical analogy: "No one would remember the Good Samaritan if he'd only had good intentions; he had money, too." Thatcher's message was that Labour might have good intentions, but unless a government focused on economics first, nothing could be achieved.

Howard admits that he has been influenced by Thatcher: "In my view, Margaret Thatcher is one of the significant political figures of Western history in the post–World War II period. It is undeniably the case that had it not been for the courage of Margaret Thatcher, the British economy would not now be one of the strongest in Europe." But for all his fawning, Howard is no Thatcher. Whether you loved or hated the Iron Lady, you have to admit that she was a politician of "courage" – the kind of leader who crashes through with bold policies in the face of strong opposition and who, as Winston Churchill said in another context, can "make the weather."

Howard is the other kind of politician, the kind who responds to the weather, constantly holding his finger in the air hoping to be the first to notice the change and to capitalise on it. The contrast in style is reflected in difference in record of achievement. Whereas Thatcher was a big reformer, Howard – despite the public perception – is not.

Hartcher explains why Howard's focus on "prosperity and security" has been such a winning formula for the Coalition. The obvious reason is that these are undoubtedly two of the most important issues facing any nation – they are naturally in the front of voters' minds when they fill out the ballot. In addition, Hartcher argues that these issues are intrinsically weighted in favour of conservatives. At the deepest level, voters identify the Liberal Party with strength and discipline and the Labor Party with softness and caring.

Hartcher believes that when it comes to security and prosperity, voters have a fundamental preference for hard noses over warm hearts. Finally, Hartcher credits Howard with being a master politician who has repeatedly turned emerging political issues to his advantage by recasting them in terms of his trump issues. In 2001 he was able to make the electorate conceive of immigration and refugees in terms of national security, and in 2007 he has already begun to convince us that climate change is a threat to economic prosperity, challenging us to recognise that action would "cost Australia jobs." For these reasons Hartcher thinks Howard will ride these issues to electoral victory.

Yet Hartcher also acknowledges that Howard's success in economics is built on luck and politics rather than achievement and policy. If Labor wishes to win the next election, it should take this message to the electorate and challenge Howard's economic dominance in three ways.

First, Labor needs to challenge Howard on where the current prosperity came from. Howard's statement that Thatcher's "achievements" are responsible for Britain's current economic strength is telling. His admiration hides an implicit admission that Australia's prosperity is due to our own contemporaneous structural transformation in the 1980s. Indeed, for several decades the Australian and British economies have followed remarkably similar trajectories. In the 1970s both countries seemed to be in terminal economic decline. Australia was afraid of becoming the "poor white trash of Asia" and Britain was derided as the "sick man of Europe."

Suddenly, along came the weather makers. Thatcher and Keating embarked on bold reform programs which wholly restructured their economies. Australia's economy was transformed from a closed "industrial museum" into a system that was "open and supple." The list of reforms in both countries (macro-economic and micro-economic) was long and deep: in Australia the currency was floated, the banking system deregulated and opened to foreigners, tariffs slashed, and the broom of competition policy brushed over every corner of the economy from airlines to supermarkets.

In both countries these monumental reforms were the bedrock for later success. But, as is often the case in politics, the party that undertook the difficult decisions was not in power when the long-term benefits were realised. John Howard and Tony Blair both inherited restructured economies with low inflation, low interest rates, declining unemployment and strong economic growth lasting more than four years. They were both, in Keating's words "hit in the arse by a rainbow."

In the last few years, Labor has made an overdue effort to reclaim the economic successes of the Hawke and Keating governments and to point out that Howard's record looks feeble by comparison. For this message to chip away at Howard's veneer of credibility, Labor needs to make it a major theme of its campaign and to enlist a wide variety of pro-reform community voices to echo the point. It also needs to demonstrate the practical effect of Howard's reform complacency: as the pace of reform has slowed, so has the pace of productivity growth – the most important economic indicator of all. Productivity growth has slowed from 2.4 per cent over the course of the 1990s to a disappointing annual rate of just over 1 per cent since 2000. In the long run, every nation's standard of living depends on its productivity. While the housing and commodity booms have made us feel richer in the short term, we are now facing a serious productivity problem.

Second, Labor needs to challenge Howard's approach to policy. Since 2005 Labor has focused its attacks on Howard around the concept of "extremism." ALP media releases are full of references to Howard's "extreme industrial relations" legislation. The word plays well in Labor's focus groups, and it has tried to tie it to Howard's economic policies, painting him as a crazed ideologue.

This strategy hasn't paid off for Labor for the simple reason that Howard is not extreme. Quite the opposite, in fact: he is extremely timid, always willing to change his mind and sacrifice his ideology at the altar of political expediency. He is much more tactically conservative than he is ideologically Conservative.

Voters know this. The electorate discovered that, despite Labor's Henny Penny protestations, the GST was a relatively minor change to the tax system which, although it made some people a little worse off, didn't lead to the Brutopia the population had been led to expect. By overstating the effect of the GST, Labor gave Howard a free kick. A negative side effect of this attempt to depict Howard as extreme is that it has reinforced Howard's claim to be a big reformer. Howard has skilfully translated extreme into bold, and painted himself as a conviction politician willing to take on the big reforms.

The ALP needs to derive a different lesson from its focus groups. It needs to point out that Howard always prioritises politics over policies, and rhetoric over reform. Howard's industrial-relations changes are an unpleasant, unfair and unnecessary step in the wrong direction. Labor needs to emphasise that these aren't a bold reform to improve the labour market, nor are they an extreme piece of ideological fervour: they are a simple attempt to crush the ALP union base and win over the small-business constituency. Labor should stop calling Howard extreme and start calling him conniving. The image of Howard as a conniving politician, willing to promote his own political expediency over any principles and the long-term future of the country, is both penetrating and accurate.

Third, Labor needs to propose a plan for the future. As citizens we want our economic cake to be increasing in size (growth), we want it to be fairly evenly distributed (equality) and we want it to be secure (risk). The economic debate between political parties is traditionally framed in terms of the first two of these issues: the Liberals are generally favoured as the party of growth, and the ALP is seen as the party of equality. If Labor is to win, it needs to broaden its image. Rudd and Swann have made good headway by outlining pro-growth policies, including programs to promote skills, innovation and infrastructure. This is a sensible agenda, but since growth has been so strong for so long, Labor has not been able to generate much interest in its alternative policies.

The third economic issue, economic security, receives a lot less attention but is of growing importance in Australia. While we have become richer in the last decade, our wealth has also become more precarious. Many families have large mortgages and credit-card bills, low savings and little job security. At the same time Howard has been pulling all the safeguards out of the system, making the labour market less secure, cutting safety nets, fuelling the house price boom and skewering organised labour.

Howard is vulnerable on economic security because he has made Australia a significantly more risky place. Jobs for life are a thing of the past, and the casual-isation of the workforce and elimination of dismissal regulations have increased the potential volatility of incomes. At the same time, savings have fallen and debt levels have risen astronomically, making households vulnerable to economic disturbances. And, as the financial side of the economy grows and more house-holds are exposed to it (more than 50 per cent of Australian adults now own shares directly, and many more are affected by the markets through their super-annuation funds), the risk of disturbances grows larger.

The effect of economic risk is already being felt in the political sphere. At the last election, highly geared voters were effectively spooked by Howard's interest-rate campaign. In the electorate with the highest proportion of mortgagees in the country, the Melbourne seat of Holt, the swing against Labor was 6 per cent, nearly three times the national average. Labor needs to capitalise on the sense of economic insecurity and make voters realise that Howard's policies are making life riskier.

A strategy with the three components outlined above will not be easy for Labor in 2007. But if it is to be competitive on economics, it must reclaim its own economic history, find a way of effectively criticising Howard's complacency in the last ten years, and articulate a vision for the new economic issues which will affect us in the next ten. If Labor does not do this, 2007 polling day will feel a bit like Groundhog Day. Howard will try to do the same this year as he did in 2004 and 2001. He will relentlessly focus on prosperity and national security, knowing that these issues are the electoral high ground and that if he can control them he can dominate the whole political landscape.

Andrew Charlton

Owen Harries

Peter Hartcher has organised his very stimulating and provocative essay around the views of two men, Donald Horne and Alan Renouf. As it happens, I knew them both and worked with each of them at different periods of my life – with Donald, editing *Quadrant* in the '60s and teaching at the University of New South Wales in the '70s; with Alan Renouf, in the Department of Foreign Affairs when he was its secretary and I was adviser to foreign minister Andrew Peacock in the Fraser government.

While both men have made contributions to Australia's understanding of itself – in Donald Horne's case an outstanding one – it seems to me that in this context they offer only limited help to Peter Hartcher in making his case.

In his section on "Luck and Leadership" Hartcher begins by quoting the key sentence from Horne's most influential book: "Australia is a lucky country run mainly by second-rate people who share its luck." But however true this was in the 1960s when *The Lucky Country* was written and published, it surely does not serve as any kind of explanation of what has happened in Australia's domestic political and economic life in the last quarter-century. As Hartcher goes on to recognise, the enormous economic success of that period was due not to luck or the behaviour of second-rate people, but to the good sense, political courage, and purposeful action of some people who, in economic terms, turned out to be "first-rate" by world standards: Hawke, Keating, Macfarlane, Howard and Costello. Moreover, their great success was due not to the adoption of novel ideas and policies, but to getting rid of some very bad existing ones and then applying some classical, well-tested remedies. As Hartcher acknowledges, because Donald Horne was temperamentally disposed to favour novelty and innovation, it took him time to appreciate the importance of what was happening.

As Hartcher also emphasises, after the Labor Party had done the hard, ground-breaking work under Hawke and Keating, it has taken ineptitude of heroic proportions for it to allow John Howard to appropriate nearly all the credit for the resulting success and to make the issue of economic prosperity his own.

In his treatment of foreign policy, Hartcher seems to accept, with no serious reservations, Renouf's thesis that Australia is, and has always been, "the frightened country." Moreover, that it is an "unreasoning fearfulness" that motivates it, one that causes it to behave "like a child." This is a pretty extreme thesis to accept uncritically, but Hartcher gets close to doing so. True, he enters a few qualifications, such as allowing that in the case of Indonesia the "menacing tones" had not always been "entirely imaginary." But in the main he agrees that throughout its history Australia has been fearful and that its fear has been irrational.

In support of this view he discusses at length Australia's early alarm at the prospect of being overrun by "Asian hordes" and its later fears of Indonesia. On the other hand, the First World War, the Second World War and the Cold War, all central events in the history of Australian foreign policy, receive very scant treatment indeed. Were these occasions when irrational fear determined Australian policy and attitudes? I suppose that it could be so argued. The main enemies and, for the most part, the main areas of conflict, were far from Australian shores. Apart from the Japanese in the Second World War, no one directly threatened our homeland with attack. In most cases Australian troops had to travel thousands of miles to participate in the fighting.

All true, but not to the point. The three great struggles of the twentieth century were conflicts concerning the central balance of the international system. In each case dissatisfied revisionist powers were concerned to challenge the existing balance, and in the case of the Second World War and the Cold War those revisionist powers had totalitarian values and goals that were inimical to those held by Australians. In each of the three cases, but especially in the last two, victory for the revisionists would have had profound adverse significance for Australia, whether we were immediately and directly attacked or not. We would have been left a weak, liberal-democratic country in an overwhelmingly hostile and menacing international environment. In those circumstances it made perfectly good sense for Australia to support Britain and the United States, the main upholders of the existing central balance, in these conflicts.

Does this then mean that the Howard government has also been right in its support for the United States in Iraq? No, it does not. This for two reasons. First, the Islamist terrorists do not threaten the central balance in the way that Nazi Germany or the Stalinist Soviet Union did, and attempts to pretend that they do are ludicrous. Second, under George W. Bush a hegemonic United States went out of its way to emphasise that its overriding concern was no longer to uphold a status quo but to alter the international system profoundly, and by force if necessary. It does not seem to me that this would serve the interest of Australia, a quintessentially satisfied, status quo country.

John Howard failed to recognise the meaning and implications of the revolutionary Bush Doctrine and proceeded to implement Australia's traditional policy in entirely altered circumstances. In doing so, and as that doctrine has deeply divided the American people, he has run the risk of converting the Australian–American alliance into an Australian–Republican Party alliance – as Howard's incredibly foolish remark that a victory for the Democrats would be a triumph for Al Qaeda made clear.

The American alliance will, and should, continue to be the centrepiece of Australian foreign policy. But this need not, and should not, imply uncritical and unqualified agreement and support on all occasions. Neither should it lead to the assumption made by Howard and Downer that the alliance constitutes anything like a watertight "security guarantee." Renouf and Hartcher are absolutely right on this point. As statesmen as diverse as Bismarck, Gladstone and Teddy Roosevelt had cause to stress, the reserve *rebus sic stantibus* – "while the same conditions apply" – is always silently understood in every treaty. In other words, no firm and unconditional guarantees are ever available in international politics.

Owen Harries

Peter Hartcher

The correspondence raises some excellent points about my essay, and it's natural that such serious analysts should overlook the essay's light-hearted opening on the subject of the canine qualities of our national leaders.

Certainly, the radio interviewers who wanted to discuss *Bipolar Nation* did not miss the opportunity to have some fun with the subject. But the dogs were there for a good reason, and it's a point that none of the correspondents has recognised.

So let me sum it up. The projective research which sought to capture voters' overall impressions of politicians by comparing them to various dog breeds makes a vital point that is borne out by the conventional polling. In assessing whether a party leader is viable, it's critical to know the electorate's impression of what sort of man he is. The research showed that there is a deeply entrenched perception of John Howard as a competent and energetic leader.

The conventional polling continues to support this. Although Rudd has enjoyed unprecedented popularity as an opposition leader, Howard has not suffered a catastrophic collapse in approval. Howard's approval rating in early May was 49 per cent in the ACNielsen poll. His rating does not approach Rudd's stratospheric support level in the 60s, but it is a sound level of support that shows that Howard remains a viable leader. This challenges the easy but fashionable assumption in early 2007 that Howard is finished, that he has been written off in the collective mind of the electorate.

What sort of enduring impression will Kevin Rudd make on the collective Australian mind? We don't yet know. His honeymoon shows distinct signs of ending, and it is not clear what will remain after the initial glow has faded. There are two points here. We know that Howard has survived Rudd's honeymoon as a viable competitor for the highest office in the land, but we cannot yet be sure how Rudd will survive his honeymoon. The portents, however, are very good.

So this is the first precondition for a party wanting to win the 2007 election – it must have a viable leader. Andrew Charlton's claim that I believe only two things matter – prosperity and security – is wrong because it ignores the centrality of a viable leader.

And while I chuckled at Bill Bowtell's wonderful image of the great necromancer John Howard reduced to the status of the Wizard of Oz – "pulling lever after lever behind a tatty curtain, mystified why nothing seems to work as well as it once did" – I disagree with his core contention that Howard is finished because of his "age, arrogance and values." It is entirely possible that Howard will lose in a contest of policies, but not because of an electoral rejection of his persona.

Indeed, Peter van Onselen reminds us of an important point – that Howard's political persona is remarkably similar to Rudd's. Both men are social conservatives. This is no coincidence. It is an expression of the fundamental nature of the Australian electorate. This helps explain why, as my essay set out, Rudd has adopted Sir Robert Menzies as his hero among Australia's former leaders.

Once the precondition of having a viable leader is met, a party that wants to win the election must satisfy two other conditions to win the confidence of the Bipolar Nation. First, a successful party must convince the electorate that it is capable of sound management of the national economy. Second, it must convince that it is capable of competently managing national security.

This is not a politically contentious point. It is a point of bipartisan consensus, and Kevin Rudd's babushka doll metaphor confirms that he didn't need me to point it out for him. Labor needs, as a basic prerequisite of credibly contesting the election, to be electorally convincing on the two outermost layers of the doll, on the economy and security.

To help explain these themes, I drew on the works of two substantial figures in Australian public policy of the past half-century. I used Donald Horne's *The Lucky Country* to set out the core economic narrative in the mind of the Bipolar Nation, and Alan Renouf's *The Frightened Country* to tell the story of national security or, more accurately, national insecurity.

Andrew Charlton takes up the question of the economic challenge Labor faces, and he should be pleased to see that the party seems to have taken his three points of advice. Rudd Labor is indeed challenging Howard on where the current prosperity came from as it seeks to reclaim its own history as the party of economic reform. It has indeed stopped calling him "extreme." It has not taken Charlton's suggestion of calling Howard "conniving," but Labor does now consistently call Howard "a clever politician." Labor is going further, and it must, to sketch out a future of sound macro-economic policy and strong productivity.

Owen Harries takes issue with Renouf's characterisation of Australia as The Frightened Country. He makes the sound point that Australia, by fighting along-side its great and powerful friends in the First World War, the Second World War and the Cold War, was actually making war in its own interest. We were fighting to defeat sinister revisionist challenges to the prevailing "Central balance."

Harries presents the Australian support for the US invasion of Iraq as an aberration. Howard had "failed to recognise the meaning and implications of the revolutionary Bush doctrine."

I beg to differ. John Howard understood exactly the implications of the Bush Doctrine. Indeed, he mimicked it with his own explicit declaration of support for pre-emption in Australia's neighbourhood. Howard proceeded with the invasion not because he misunderstood it, but because he decided to value the alliance *über alles*.

Why would Howard put overriding priority on the US alliance, even though it was a decision that broke with Australian history and Australian interests as a status quo power? It was precisely because Howard agrees with the fundamental precept of Australians as a people uneasy about our national security, and a people who, therefore, place tremendous hope and faith in the enduring vision of a saving alliance. This is not a question of policy so much as a matter of national psychology.

Note the stark strategic divergence between Australia and its close neighbour New Zealand in the last three decades. New Zealand dreams of itself as a pacifist country that rejects the US alliance, runs down its war-fighting capability, and deploys forces only for peacekeeping and humanitarian purposes.

By contrast, Australia sees itself as an active participant in global power politics, a staunch ally of the US, with a combat capability ready to defend the interests of the country and its ally. Why?

The core reason is national psychology and threat perception. New Zealand thinks of itself as a Western Pacific country protected from the world by the reassuring bulk of the continent of Australia. We, by contrast, think of ourselves as a frontline state confronting a suspiciously alien Indonesia.

Rudd Labor has made great progress in pegging back Howard's advantage as the perceived better manager of national prosperity and national security. He has not yet neutralised the government on either. With some six months to the election, it is an open contest. Yet it should send chills down the Labor spine that, despite the greatest honeymoon of any opposition leader in the 35-year series of the ACNielsen poll, Howard has held onto his advantage in both areas.

Peter Hartcher

**Bill Bowtell** was senior political adviser to the Prime Minister of Australia between 1994 and 1996. As senior adviser to the federal health minister, he played a significant role in the introduction of the Medicare health insurance system and was an architect of Australia's successful and well-regarded response to HIV/AIDS.

**Andrew Charlton** is a research economist at the London School of Economics and the co-author, with Joseph Stiglitz, of *Fair Trade for All* (2005). His book *Ozonomics: Inside the Myth of Australia's Economic Superheroes* will be published later this year.

**Owen Harries** is a senior fellow at the Centre for Independent Studies and a visiting fellow at the Lowy Institute for International Policy. From 1985 to 2000 he was editor of *The National Interest* in Washington DC.

**Peter Hartcher** is the political and international editor for the *Sydney Morning Herald* and was until 2004 the Washington bureau chief of the *Australian Financial Review*. In 1996 he received the Gold Walkley Award. He is the author of two books, *The Ministry* and *Bubble Man*, and a visiting fellow at the Lowy Institute for International Policy.

**David Marr** is the author of *Patrick White: a Life* and *The High Price of Heaven*, and wrote *Dark Victory* with Marian Wilkinson. In a career spanning more than thirty years, he has written for the *National Times* and the *Bulletin*, been a reporter for *Four Corners* and, until recently, presenter of ABC-TV's *Media Watch*. He now writes for the *Sydney Morning Herald*.

**Peter van Onselen** is a senior lecturer in political science at Edith Cowan University in Perth and co-author with Wayne Errington of *John Winston Howard: The Biography*, to be published in August. His book on the 2007 federal election will be published next year.

www.ingramcontent.com/pod-product-compliance
Lightning Source LLC
Chambersburg PA
CBHW061238270326
41930CB00026B/3498